PROJECT MANAGEMENT INSTITUTE

IDENTIFYING THE FORCES DRIVING FREQUENT CHANGE IN PMOS

Monique Aubry, PhD, MPM, and **Brian Hobbs**, PhD, MBA, PMP
School of Business and Management
University of Quebec at Montreal

Ralf Müller, DBA, MBA, PMP
Umeå School of Business, Umeå University
BI Norwegian School of Management

Tomas Blomquist, PhD
Umeå School of Business, Umeå University

Library of Congress Cataloging-in-Publication Data:

Identifying the forces driving frequent change in PMOs / Monique Aubry ... [et al.].
   p. cm.
ISBN 978-1-935589-31-0 (pbk. : alk. paper) 1. Project management. 2. Organizational
change. I. Aubry, Monique.
HD69.P75I34 2011
658.4'04—dc23

2011029626

ISBN: 978-1-935589-31-0

Published by: Project Management Institute, Inc.
                  14 Campus Boulevard
                  Newtown Square, Pennsylvania 19073-3299 USA.
                  Phone: +610-356-4600
                  Fax: +610-356-4647
                  E-mail: customercare@pmi.org
                  Internet: www.PMI.org

PMI Publications welcomes corrections and comments on its books. Please feel free to
send comments on typographical, formatting, or other errors. Simply make a copy of the
relevant page of the book, mark the error, and send it to: Book Editor, PMI Publications,
14 Campus Boulevard, Newtown Square, PA 19073-3299 USA.

To inquire about discounts for resale or educational purposes, please contact the PMI
Book Service Center.

        PMI Book Service Center
        P.O. Box 932683, Atlanta, GA 31193-2683 USA
        Phone:1-866-276-4764 (within the U.S. or Canada) or +1-770-280-4129 (globally)
        Fax: +1-770-280-4113
        E-mail: book.orders@pmi.org

10 9 8 7 6 5 4 3 2 1

ACKNOWLEDGMENTS

The authors would like to thank PMI and the Per and Eivor Wikström Foundation for their financial support. They also wish to express their gratitude to all those who participated in this research: the seventeen organizations and their employees for their time and interest participating in case studies, the PMI Montreal Chapter's Community of Practice on PMOs, GP Quebec (the public sector community of practice of the Quebec Government), several PMI local chapters, and colleagues from the University of Limerick, Athabasca University, and ESC-Lille. The authors also wish to thank Carl St-Pierre, who provided invaluable assistance in both the preparation of the survey instruments and the analysis of data. Partial results have been presented, discussed and enriched in many different venues during the three years this research project has unfolded. The authors thank all the participants who took part in these conversations. Correspondence concerning this article should be addressed to Monique Aubry, School of Business and Management, University of Quebec at Montreal, Montreal (Quebec), H3C 3P8, Canada. Email: aubry. monique@uqam.ca.

TABLE OF CONTENTS

LIST OF FIGURES

LIST OF TABLES

EXECUTIVE SUMMARY

Previous research has shown that PMOs change frequently (Hobbs & Aubry, 2010). The objective of this research is to better understand the frequent transformations of PMOs. The unit of analysis in this research is a transformation of a PMO: a situation where an existing PMO is transformed into a new PMO with a different structure and/or a different role in the organization. The object of study is a change process, which has been modeled as shown in Figure 2.2, reproduced here. The research focuses on the drivers of the change, the nature of the change and its impacts.

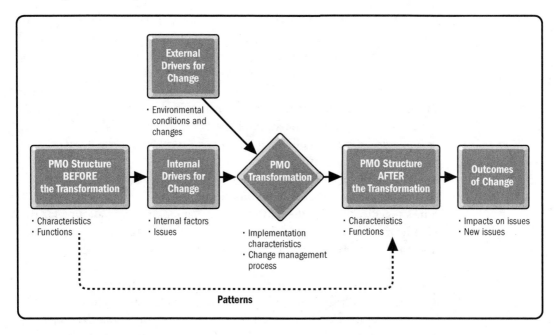

Figure 2.2. Conceptual Framework for a PMO Transformation

The research was conducted in two major phases: (1) 17 qualitative case studies of a transformation of PMOs and (2) a survey to investigate a larger number of PMO transformations.

In a previous research project, seven in-depth qualitative case studies of PMO transformations were undertaken (Hobbs & Aubry, 2010; Aubry, 2007). The results of this research provided the starting point for the present research. An additional 10 case studies were conducted (five in Canada and five in Sweden). The objective of the additional case studies was to gain greater insight into the phenomena being studied and to develop and refine the survey instrument for the quantitative study in Phase Two. Preliminary versions of the questionnaire were used during the 10 additional case studies and comments and suggestions on improving the questionnaire were sought in each case. The result was a survey instrument that has been thoroughly validated.

The survey instrument is based on the same conceptual model and consists of questions related to the same concepts: drivers of change, descriptions of PMOs before and after the change, and impacts of the change. Information on the organizational context was also gathered on a sample of 184 PMO transformations.

The key findings from the qualitative case studies are:

1. The analysis of the qualitative case studies confirms that the conceptual framework captures the transformation process and helps in understanding the phenomenon. In this research, the focus has been put on one transformation, but the process should be understood as a continuous dynamic. It calls for a systemic circular thinking where consequences become the conditions for the next cycle.
2. A total of 32 drivers of PMO transformations were identified: five types of events external to the organization, nine events internal to the organization and eighteen issues or debates that drove changes to PMOs. PMO transformations are triggered primarily by the internal dynamics of the organization.
3. Multiple simultaneous external or internal events or both participate in the change, as do internal issues. Transformations are not triggered by a single driver. It confirms that the PMO is part of multiple social, political, and technological systems. Political tensions seem to prevail at the interface with the rest of the organization.
4. Reconfiguration of a PMO is not random. On the contrary, the resulting PMO becomes aligned with the organizational context. A particular set of characteristics comes together to form the new PMO configuration. One indicator for this alignment can be seen in the relative stability of the configuration up to a point where a certain level of misalignment leads to a change.

The key findings from the survey's descriptive statistics are:

1. Responses on PMO demographics showed similarity with earlier studies (Hobbs & Aubry, 2010). PMOs in particular organizations are changing every few years but the characteristics of the overall population of PMOs are not changing very quickly.
2. Changes in PMOs are significant and their implementation is apparently quite difficult.
3. Although a PMO transformation is a significant organizational change, only about 50% are implemented using an organizational change management process to accompany the transformation.
4. Multiple events and issues play a role in the PMO transition. No single driver is at a higher level of importance. This reinforces the assumption of the interweaving of multiple reasons that lead to a PMO change.

The key findings from the principal component analysis and correlation analysis are:

1. The case studies identified (a) large number of reasons why PMOs are changed; (b) changes that are made to PMOs; and (c) impacts of these changes. The descriptive statistics showed that most or all of these variables were important. It is difficult to draw conclusions from the variety of information presented therein. The factor analysis identified underlying patterns that reduced this great variety to a small number of factors for each of these groups of variables.

2. All five of the external contextual variables were grouped into one factor with no variables excluded from the analysis. All of the variables relate to changes in the economic or institutional context or both.

3. Change in top management was the only factor that was identified related to events and conditions within the organization. Change in top management was related to broad organizational change. The several examples of changes in top management were all related, indicating that such changes tend not to be isolated events but to form a pattern of general structural change in the organization.

4. Many issues can drive changes to PMOs. The factor analysis found an underlying structure of four factors:
   a. Portfolio management and methods
   b. Collaboration and accountability
   c. Project management maturity and performance
   d. Work climate.

5. PMOs are complex entities. Changing a PMO can mean changing many different things. The factor analysis identified an underlying structure of four different types of changes made to PMOs. The most important was changes to the roles or functions filled by the PMO. The analysis was quite efficient in that it only put two design variables aside: accountability for scope, costs and schedule and for benefits. It would seem that despite the great number of possible changes that can be made to PMOs, there is an underlying pattern among the organizational choices being made that reduces these choices considerably.

6. Changes to PMOs produce impacts on the organization. These impacts were evaluated in this study by the degree of improvement or deterioration in the issues that are related to changes in PMOs. Not surprisingly, when a PMO is changed because of an issue there is a tendency to find an improvement in that issue.

7. The analysis failed to reveal a pattern among the factors. Conditions and issues driving changes to PMOs were generally not related to the actual changes made to the PMOs. Organizational reality is plausibly too complex and too subtle to reveal simple relationships whereby a particular condition or issue would lead to a particular change in the PMO.

8. The examination of associations between contextual variables and the issues, changes and impacts associated with PMO transitions did not identify many significant patterns. There were only two significant findings. First, large organizations doing projects for internal customers see portfolio management and methods as more important issues, which is an intuitive result. Second, more mature organizations see maturity and performance as more important issues. This is somewhat surprising at first glance, but is consistent with a mature process for continuous improvement.

9. Several associations were identified between the process for implementing changes to PMOs and the drivers of change, the nature of the changes being implemented and the improvements that were delivered. This highlights both the importance of questions related to implementation and to the variability found among organizations in this regard.

Further attempt to identify patterns in the PMO transformation process has been undertaken using the analysis of mediator and moderator effects. The key findings are:

1. The analysis of mediating and moderating effects did not reveal important general patterns among the variables in the form of particular drivers of change leading to specific changes in PMO and in turn to specific improvements. However, some significant findings did shed light on specific situations.

2. The pattern that leads most directly to guidelines for managerial practice is that when portfolio management and methods are important issues, decreases in the scope and controlling nature of the PMO's mandate are associated with greater improvements on these issues.

3. Making significant changes to a PMO is an organizational change and should be managed as such.

4. Project management maturity does not have a direct effect on organizational improvements. It does have moderator effects in some situations. This may reflect the effect of the monitoring, management and continuous improvement functions found at higher levels of maturity.

Conclusion

It was possible in the seventeen case studies to understand how the context had unfolded and how the drivers led to the changes that were made to the PMO. No significant general patterns were identified. The analysis did reveal some very partial patterns and some rather complex interactions. These were not enough to identify general patterns but were illustrative of the complex interactions occurring during the transformation process.

The failure to identify general patterns in the transformation process suggests the question, "Why?" There may be several explanations but the most salient are:

1. The transformation of a particular PMO is driven by a complex set of drivers that become salient over time in a particular organizational context. The organizational dynamics that lead to a transformation of a PMO may be so context-specific that it is not possible to identify which drivers lead to which changes in the PMO independently from the context.

2. Methodologically, it is very difficult if not impossible to capture a complex social, organizational and political process such as a transformation of a PMO using a survey.

CHAPTER ONE: INTRODUCTION

1.1 Context of this Research

Project management has come to play a central role in the management of organizations in almost all fields of human activity. Bredillet, Ruiz, and Yatim (2008) reported from World Bank data that 21% of the world's gross domestic product (GDP) is gross capital formation, which is tightly related to project activities. This is also reflected within organizations where a greater portion of their activities is organized by projects. Over the last decade, many organizations have implemented one or more Project Management Offices (PMOs) as part of organizational project management, attributing a variety of both operational and strategic roles to their PMOs (Dai & Wells, 2004). While PMOs are now a prominent feature of organizational project management, the underlying logical argument that leads to their implementation or renewal is still not fully understood.

People responsible for establishing or managing a PMO have a great variety of options with respect to both the organizational structures and the functions within the mandate of the PMO. In addition, executives ask for value from these structures and PMO managers are often hard-pressed to show value for money. The current state of knowledge of PMOs and how they contribute to value creation provides PMO managers with very few resources. The practitioner community is looking for standards, or at least guidelines, to help them and their executives to be more successful in establishing and managing PMOs. On the other hand, the project management research community is looking for recognition of its theoretical base within the larger management research community. An international effort has been made recently to formalize theoretical knowledge in the field of project management with the identification of nine schools of thought (Bredillet, 2007). Research on PMOs relates more specifically to the Governance School (Bredillet, 2008). The research presented in this paper will contribute to theoretical knowledge not only on the PMO but more largely to organizational project management and its dynamic context.

Many consultants and some researchers have written on PMOs in recent years. The focus of the vast majority of this work has been on identifying the characteristics of PMOs and a limited number of variables that would drive the configurations of new or existing PMOs. The implicit underlying assumptions in the current literature are that there are a limited number of variations of PMOs and that PMOs are relatively stable structural entities. However, results of a survey of 500 PMOs documented a great variety and lack of consensus on their value, their structure, and the functions included in their mandate (Hobbs & Aubry, 2007).

On the other hand, at least three independent surveys have shown that the average age of PMOs is approximately two years (Hobbs & Aubry, 2007; Interthink Consulting, 2002; Stanleigh, 2005). This has not changed in recent years. The authors know of no research results that are inconsistent with these observations. Therefore, PMOs are often not stable structures but temporary arrangements with a rather short life expectancy.

In the same vein, the case studies conducted by Dr. Aubry as part of her doctoral thesis (Aubry, 2007) illustrated the temporary nature of PMOs. This case study research revealed that significant changes in PMOs can be associated with changes in senior management personnel, their organizational or strategic vision, or both. The case study results indicate that a more fruitful approach for future research would be to focus on the organizational change process surrounding the implementation or the transformation of a PMO, rather than focusing on the characteristics of the PMO as a static organizational entity. The pertinence of this process approach to a better understanding of PMOs has been validated in the context of executive workshops held in Canada, the United States, Australia and Europe.

Following recommendation for future research, the present research addresses the organizational change process surrounding the transformation of a PMO. Results presented in this monograph come from two sources of data: 17 case studies and 184 responses to a questionnaire. Both have been orchestrated in a global methodological strategy. Results illustrate the temporary nature of PMOs and reveal that significant changes in PMOs can be associated with the organization's internal or external environment.

In light of the current organizational context described above, the high-level objective of this research is to understand the forces that are driving the frequent reconfigurations of PMOs. More specifically, this research intends to answer these questions:

- Why do PMOs change? What are the drivers?
- How does the change happen? Is there a dynamic change process?
- What is changing? What are the characteristics or functions that are changing?
- Is there any pattern of change?

Results from this research should contribute to building the theoretical foundations of project management more specifically in the Governance School. It should also provide guidance to project management practitioners and upper management executives in the implementation, remodeling and management of PMOs.

1.2 The Origin of this Research

This monograph aims at providing an in-depth understanding of the PMO transformation process. It delivers the results from a three-year research project specifically dedicated to changes affecting PMOs. This research was undertaken as a continuous effort from the earlier stages of a research program on PMOs within the Project Management Research Chair at the University of Quebec at Montreal (UQAM; www.pmchair.uqam.ca). In 2003 and 2004, this research program was launched in order to develop a better understanding of this important phenomenon.

The objectives of the research program are twofold. The first objective is to produce a reliable description of the present population of PMOs. The second objective is to develop a better understanding of PMOs, why they take on such a variety of forms, and the dynamics surrounding their creation, transformation, and action in organizations. As shown in Table 1.1, the research program includes six phases, with this specific research corresponding to Phase V.

Table 1.1. Research Program on PMOs at UQAM

Phase of the Research Program	Period	Description
1	2005-2006	Two descriptive surveys of 500 PMOs aimed at providing a realistic portrait of the population of PMOs.
2	2006	The development of a rich conceptual model to guide further investigation.
3	2006-2007	In-depth case studies of 12 PMOs in 4 organizations aimed at understanding the dynamics surrounding PMOs in their organizational context.
4	2008	Analysis of the data from phases I, II & III and production of a monograph published by PMI
5	**2008-2010**	**Identifying the forces driving the frequent changes in PMOs**
6	2009-2011	Governance and communities of PMOs

Over the last several years, many conversations at professional congresses and workshops have revealed a negative interpretation of frequent PMO transformations. A PMO change is often considered the result of a failure or a deficiency in the PMO. Thus, a new configuration of the PMO, one may think, should correct the fault and last forever, though this is rarely the case. From this perspective, multiple failures lead to a loss of legitimacy and confidence in the PMO and sometimes in the global project management approach.

During the in-depth case studies of 12 PMOs in Phase III of the research program, the idea of a process of PMO transformation came up prominently in interviews (see Aubry, 2007). While the questionnaire for semi-structured interviews asked for a description of the evolution of the PMO structure, respondents' replies described how they have understood the transformation of their PMO. In-depth analysis of interview transcripts in a grounded theory approach offered a first understanding of PMO transformation in terms of a continuous process.

This research has emerged from divergent perspectives on the reasons why PMOs are changing so often. On one side, changes are seen as the result of a failure on the part of the PMO. On the other side, change is seen as simply a natural periodic phenomenon.

This research has the particularity of being realized in collaboration with Umeå School of Business, Umeå University, Sweden. Aubry was a post-doctoral researcher at Umeå School of Business. This collaboration translated into rich case studies and, more significantly, cross-fertilization of ideas throughout the research.

CHAPTER TWO: LITERATURE REVIEW AND CONCEPTUAL FRAMEWORK

"The organization that never changes eventually loses synchronization with its environment, while the one that never stabilizes can produce no product or service efficiently. Accordingly, there is always change embedded in the stability of an organization, just as there is always stability embedded in its change. Some things must remain fixed as other things shift. " (Mintzberg & Westley, 1992, p. 46)

It is not difficult to capture the PMO's reality in a snapshot. What is difficult is to make sense of the pace of its transformation. As Mintzberg and Westley (1992) suggest, organizational change is a necessary feature in every organization. The PMO is no exception to this rule. In this context, we intend to review the literature on PMOs and organizational change and to propose a conceptual framework that will help make sense of the PMO's transformation process. Change is defined as the act, process or result of changing. Similarly, transformation is defined as an act, process or instance of transforming or being transformed (Merriam-Webster, 2007). In this monograph we use the terms change and transformation interchangeably.

In the first section, the authors explore the PMO in the current literature and end with a proposal for an empirically-validated PMO model. In the second section, the authors delve into the organizational structure. In the third section, they address organizational change. Finally, based on this review, the authors propose in the fourth section a conceptual framework for understanding the PMO's transformation process.

2.1 The PMO in the Literature

2.1.1 Definition of the PMO and Standardization

A Guide to the Project Management Body of Knowledge (PMBOK® Guide) defines a PMO as:

> *An organizational body or entity assigned various responsibilities related to the centralized and coordinated management of those projects under its domain. The responsibilities of the PMO can range from providing project management support functions to actually being responsible for the direct management of a project.* (Project Management Institute, 2008a, p. 435)

This definition is very close to the definition the authors adopted for this investigation in that it highlights the fact that PMOs are organizational entities and that their mandates vary significantly from one organization to another. However, the present study makes a distinction between the multi-project PMO and the single-project PMO or "project office," which is responsible for the management of one large project. The *PMBOK® Guide* definition and much of the literature on PMOs include both, and both are important phenomena worthy of investigation. However, the two are also quite different and can best be investigated separately. The scope of the present investigation includes only PMOs with mandates that cover many projects, or multi-project PMOs.

In part because of the great variety found among PMOs in different organizations, and in part because of the lack of a consensus among practitioners and adequate descriptions in the literature, discussions on this topic tend to be characterized by diversity of opinion and confusion. Many people have been exposed to a limited number of PMOs and have concluded inappropriately that all PMOs are similar to the ones they have observed. The lack of consensus is understandable given (1) that the PMO is a relatively recent phenomenon, (2) that PMOs take on a great variety of forms and functions, and (3) that there has been a lack of systematic investigation. The present study uses a rather broad definition of the PMO in order to capture the variety of form and function. For the purposes of this study, it is not necessary for the organizational unit to be called a PMO.

The emergence of and the need for the PMO are associated with the increasing number and complexity of projects throughout the business world, which have led to a certain form of centralization (Dai & Wells, 2004; Marsh, 2000). Nearly 75 unique functions have been identified (Crawford, 2004). Some authors see PMOs playing an active role in specific functions. Huemann and Anbari (2007) stated that PMOs should be more involved in audit functions, particularly in what is learned from audits, and Hueman, Keegan and Turner (2007) identified the PMO as a key factor in human resources management in project-oriented organizations. However, the reality of PMOs is highly divergent.

References to PMOs are relatively plentiful in the professional literature (Benko & McFarlan, 2003; Bridges & Crawford, 2001; Crawford, 2002; Crawford & Cabanis-Brewin, 2006; Dinsmore, 1999; Duggal, 2001; Goncalves, 2006; Hatfield, 2008; Kendall & Rollins, 2003; Perry, 2009) but limited in the scientific literature. Texts from the professional literature deal principally with three themes: the justification of the PMO's existence, its roles or functions, and steps for its implementation. The descriptions of PMOs in this literature are often summarized in typologies comprised of a small number of models. The most common types of PMOs described in the literature proposed three or four models (see Table 2.1). The Gartner Research Group's study (cited in Kendall & Rollins, 2003) proposed one of the most influential typologies of PMOs. The Gartner Group typology is comprised of three types of PMOs: (1) project repository, (2) coach, and (3) enterprise.

Table 2.1. PMO Models from Current Literature

Author	Single Project	Multiple-Project Entities			
Dinsmore (1999)	Autonomous Project Team	Project Support Office	PM Center of Excellence	Program Management	
Gartner Group, Light (2000)		Project Repository	Coach	Enterprise	
Crawford (2002)	Level 1 Project Control Office	Level 2 Business Unit Project Office	Level 3 Strategic Project Office		
Englund et al. (2003)		Project Support Office	PM Center of Excellence	Program Management Office	
Kendall & Rollins (2003)		Project Repository	Coach	Enterprise	Deliver now

Some of the typologies identify the single-project entity of "project office," which is outside the scope of the present study. Each of the typologies proposes two, three, or four multi-project PMOs, organized in an ascending hierarchy. The PMO progression is intended to follow an incremental path from a low-level to a high-level model. Some authors proposed a maturity model specific for PMOs (Kendall & Rollins, 2003) where the same assumption of progression is taken for granted. The picture that emerges from our case studies does not support a regular progression toward a better PMO.

Recent research on PMOs looks at performance or value creation. A first empirical study didn't conclude any strong findings on PMO performance (Dai & Wells, 2004). More recently, two papers proposed radically different perspectives on the value created by PMOs. First, Hurt and Thomas (2009) proposed the concept of sustainability to capture the idea of the PMO maintaining its value over time through PMO changes. Second, Pellegrinelli and Garagna (2009) suggested the concept of the emptying process to describe the phenomenon of transferring knowledge from the PMO to the rest of the organization leading to the PMO's dismantlement (Pellegrinelli & Garagna, 2009). Another avenue to explore the PMO's performance would be to turn to multiple views of the contribution of the PMO to organizational performance (Aubry & Hobbs, 2010).

In the face of such diversity among PMOs and the absence of consensus for developing standards, some professional organizations propose frameworks to help their members support their organization. Having participated in local and international communities of practices related to PMOs, the authors are sensitive to requests from professionals who are frequently asked to help implement or restructure a PMO. It is natural that they turn to their professional association for answers. The Program Management Office Specific Interest Group (PMOSIG) within PMI has answered these requests by publishing a book containing papers that present successful practices tested by its members (PMOSIG, 2008, 2010). The UK Office of Government Commerce has complemented their best practice guidance with a book specifically about offices, whether at the project, program or portfolio level (Office of Government Commerce, 2008).

2.1.2 PMO Descriptive Model

This model describes the PMO using sets of characteristics and functions. This model has been developed using 500 descriptions of PMOs from a survey that was done in 2005 (Hobbs & Aubry, 2010). The sets of characteristics are grouped into four classes: organizational context, PMO structural characteristics, roles or functions of the PMO and performance of the PMO (see Figure 2.1). The complete list of elements within these four classes of data is presented in Appendix A.

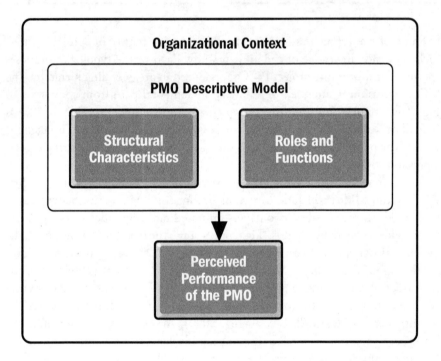

Figure 2.1. PMO Model

Organizational context. The organizational context is described using two different classes of data: organizational characteristics and the types of projects in the mandate. Organizational characteristics include characteristics that are often used in the organizational literature such as the economic sector, public or private, and size of the organization. More specific to project-based organizations are elements referring to the matrix structure, the project management maturity level and the supportiveness of the organizational culture. The types of projects an organization undertakes may have an impact on the configuration of the PMO. Projects can be divided into types in many different ways (Crawford, Hobbs & Turner, 2005).

The PMO structural characteristics. The description of a PMO is at the heart of a PMO model. Two classes of variables are proposed to capture their structural characteristics and the functions they perform. The structural characteristics cover a variety of elements, including the name used to identify the entity, location in the organization, level of decision-making authority, characteristics of the staff, and the percentage of projects and of project managers within the PMO.

The population of PMOs can best be described as varied in all structural characteristics. When setting up a PMO or reconfiguring an existing PMO, there are a wide variety of options, and different organizations make very different choices. One of the most significant illustrations of this variety is the choice of whether to place project managers within the PMO; almost half have all or most of the organization's project managers located within their structures and the other half have no or very few project managers.

The roles or functions of the PMO. PMOs fill many different organizational functions. The model proposes nine basic groups of functions. An original list of 27 functions was produced and validated in the first phase of the research program. This list was reduced to the nine presented here through both statistical and conceptual analyses. Each group was examined to ensure that it was internally consistent in both conceptual and practical terms. The list of nine was further validated during the case studies of Phase 3 of the research program (Hobbs & Aubry, 2010).

These groups show the structure underlying the many functions fulfilled by PMOs in organizations. Identifying groups of functions that are both conceptually and statistically sound has very practical consequences. The long and disorganized list of functions is replaced by a simple structure of underlying high-level functions. All of these groups of functions are important for a significant number of PMOs and none can be excluded from consideration. When organizations set up a PMO or reconfigure an existing PMO, they choose the functions to include in the PMO's mandate from a list of possible functions. Different organizations choose different combinations of functions, thus creating a variety of PMOs.

The PMO, whatever its characteristics and roles or the functions it performs, is by definition part of the organizational structure dedicated to project management. The following section provides different perspectives on organizational structures.

2.2 Organizational Structure

Mintzberg (1989) proposed a clear and simple definition of a structure as "the total of the ways in which its labor is divided into distinct tasks and then its coordination achieved among those tasks (p.100)." The PMO fits quite well in this definition as a coordination locus of project tasks. However, the PMO is embedded in various combinations within the parent organization (Hobbs & Aubry, in press).

Today's organizations face major challenges about how they are structured, how they are organized and how technology is involved. Organizational structures have developed over time and new structures have emerged (Pettigrew, 2003). Structures are often more hybrid-like: distributed, dependent on networks of other organizations (Powell, 1990), N-Form (Hedlund, 1994), molecular (Morabito, Sack, & Bhate, 1999), cellular (Miles, Snow, Mathews, Miles, & Coleman, 1997), arranged in strategic allegiance (Eisenhardt & Schoonhoven, 1996), customer-centric (Galbraith, 2002), and changed in concordance with technological changes (e.g., Ciborra, 1996). But these new forms of organizing build upon an existing hierarchy. Continuity exists in traditional hierarchical forms of organizing. New characteristics are simply added on to the existing hierarchy (Ruigrok, Pettigrew, Peck, & Whittington, 1999).

While functions continue to play an important role, this role is changing with the increasing use of project-based forms of organizing and investments in cross-functional management skills. An indication of these changes can be seen in the fact that hybrid structures of program and project portfolios have better performance than traditional forms where the two are separated (Blomquist & Müller, 2006). Scholars of configurations (Mintzberg, 1979; Miller & Friesen, 1982) suggest that there are a number of designs or structures. It is clear that new structures have evolved as organizations work more in networks, as Powell (1990) shows, or as organizations work more across different national borders, as discussed by Nohria and Ghoshal (1997). The use of information technology can also have an impact on structure (Schwarz & Brock, 1998). But one prevalent fact is that hybrid structures are common.

The complexity of structure in many contemporary organizations today is also illustrated by Blomquist and Müller (2006) where program and portfolio managers often have an integrated role between different structures in order to manage projects. The complexity of the organizational structure has increased in the traditional ways of looking at R&D, production and sales. But of interest in this study is the fact that the complexity has also influenced the organizational structure, particularly in how organizations structure and organize projects in programs, portfolios and PMOs.

The study of organizational structures has interested scholars within the innovation field who are interested in what structures would better encourage innovation. For example, Burns and Stalker (1961) argue that a more *organic* solution has to be adopted when uncertainty is high and the environment unstable. Another approach is based upon a classification from J. G. March (1991), where activities undertaken within organizations can be classified under exploration and operation. Operations take place in a more functional and stable context, such as hierarchy, while activities of exploration refer to new tasks that would benefit from flexible arrangements (Hedlund, 1994).

In the more specific field of project management, structures have been studied mostly in relation to the parent organization from pure functional to strong matrix and network organizations (Hobbs & Ménard, 1993; Hobday, 2000; Larson, 2004). Shenhar and Dvir (2004) have shown that three parameters that differentiate project types have an impact on structure: uncertainty, complexity, and development pace.

In conclusion, structures and the process of structuring have been discussed over the last few decades (for a review, see Sminia, 2009). Clearly, structuring is closely linked to organizational changes, transformation and the dynamics of the organization following Pettigrew (1990) or Giddens (1984). Pettigrew (2003) proposed the term strategizing-structuring to highlight the dynamic and close relationship between strategy and structure. We will also follow this path and move into the literature of organizational change.

2.3 Organizational Change

The aim of this research is to understand *why* and *how* PMOs are changing. A comprehensive review of the literature on organizational changes is outside the scope of this monograph. In the following section, the focus will be on the organization level.

2.3.1 Contingency Theory

The historical perspective on organizational change suggests an evolution in the understanding of this phenomenon from the contingency approach towards the dynamic systems approach. Changes in organizations were first interpreted as a contingent response to external events (Chandler, 1962, 1980). Contingency theory claims that there is no single best organization structure, because structures and other organizational design factors vary, contingent on the organization's environmental factors (Donaldson, 1996). The contingency theory developed from the classic studies of Burns and Stalker (1961), which identified mechanistic and organic structures as appropriate for stable and unstable organizational environments. The basic tenet of the contingency theory is that organizations perform better if their structure is aligned with their environment. Possible environmental factors influencing design decisions are manifold. Donaldson (1996) refers to a two-stage model with task uncertainty as the first order construct and innovativeness and size as second order constructs. These impact the decision for appropriate control structures, which, in turn, lead to mechanistic or organic structures. Other factors, however, should not be ignored, such as the life-cycle states of an organization's products and the associated skills and resource requirements for the related product development projects. Donaldson (1985) identified 16 different structural designs for the management of the interactions between projects in multi-project and multi-product organizations. Further developments of this theory took into account a critique of the one-dimensionality of this theory, stating that not only do environments shape organizations, but organizations shape environments. This led to the refinement of the contingency theory aiming for "structural adjustment to regain fit" (Donaldson, 1987), which assumes that the ultimate cause of structural change is a change in the contingency variable. From this perspective, Donaldson (1987) argued that:

> [...] the need for structural change arises from the substandard performance which comes from the mismatch of structure and contingency (i.e., the misfit between the new value of the contingency variable and the old structure) rather than just from the change in the value of the contingency variable (pp. 2-3).

Contingency theory has been prominent in the field of organizational analysis since the mid-1970s (Donaldson, 2001). The idea that organizations adapt to their context has become part of the common sense of studying and managing organizations. The development of the PMO and its structure has been studied by Hobbs and Aubry (2010). Their findings indicate that several of the organizational contextual variables that are found in the contingency theory literature show little or no systematic variation with the characteristics of PMOs. The explanation of this apparent paradox is quite simple; many organizational contextual variables are more stable than PMOs, most of which change significantly every two to three years. If one variable is changing quickly and the other is changing slowly or remaining stable, one would not expect to find any systematic association between them. This research is not the first to find a lack of relationship between contingency factors and organizational phenomena. Historically, contingency factors such as size of the firm or industrial sector are not determining factors for understanding innovation or performance among firms (Zeitlin, 2008).

Contingency theory still contributes to the understanding of organizational change (see Chapter Seven). On the other hand, organizations are seen as active participants within larger dynamic systems (Hughes, 1987). In this perspective, changes are the norm instead of the exception. We first explored, through the literature, the reasons *why* organizations change, by looking at the drivers for change. In the next sub-section, organizational changes are explored from a process view, to understand *how* change occurs.

2.3.2 The Evolutionary Perspective

A complementary view on organizational change is found in the evolutionary perspective. This allows the authors to consider the context and the historical anchorage of the change within the parent organization.

Organizational change mobilized much attention from economic scholars after Schumpeter recognized organizational innovations as part of the creative destruction process (Schumpeter, 1950). Evolutionary theory developed within the Schumpeterian tradition to better understand technological change at the macro-level (long economic cycle), but scholars also brought their attention to bear on the micro-level, opening the black box of routines, learning and innovation within organizations (Lévesque, Bourque, & Forgues, 2001). The basic evolutionary model envisions the organization as a collection of routines or stable bundles of activities. With time, variation occurs within these routines with the result that any given set of routines evolves, whether intentionally or not. A certain number of new routines are then adopted as temporarily permanent practices.

This simple pattern of "variation – selection – retention" repeats continuously (Miner, 1994). Within evolutionary theory, organizational change is seen as a continuous process. It is viewed as the action of changing, in reference to Weick, who called for action verbs in language instead of names (Pettigrew, Woodman, & Cameron, 2001). Path dependency conditions the organizational trajectory due to the irreversibility of investment. Yet organizational context and history remain important for understanding organizational change.

The capacity of organizations to change their routines and structures has already been pinpointed as a source of competitiveness (Pettigrew, 2003). Conversely, within the evolutionary theory, inertia in large organizations has been identified as a constraint for organizations to succeed in their competitive environment. Innovation studies and evolutionary economics have widely explored the relation between organizational characteristics and changes at the organizational level and knowledge management and technological innovation activities at the population level (Massini, Lewin, Numagami, & Pettigrew, 2002, p.1134). Researchers embracing the evolutionary theory have linked together multiple levels of analysis to explain complex phenomena (Hughes, 1987; Massini et al., 2002; Van de Ven & Garud, 1994). This approach allowed for the inclusion of interactions between levels of analysis taking into account multiple interacting processes crossing boundaries (Pettigrew et al., 2001).

The aim of this research is to open up the PMO's *black box* at the moment when change occurred. The focus is therefore placed at the organizational level and explores the process of PMO change. Following Massini et al. (2002), "the level of analysis in evolutionary economics is normally the firm, within which tacit and explicit forms of knowledge interact and are selected on the bases of choices made by individuals, according to some utility emerging from the historical and economic context" (p. 1335). This gives the opportunity to observe routines that are changing in relation to their context. The PMO can be described as a structural entity embedding a bundle of routines using the PMO descriptive model.

In this specific research, the unit of analysis is the PMO transformation at one point in time. Within the evolutionary perspective, this unique transformation is part of a continuous movement; conditions of the PMO transformation are the result of previous contexts or culture. It also allows for the observation of multiple levels of analysis and their interactions.

2.3.3 Patterns of Change

Patterns of change have long been discussed and there is no pretense of describing the entire field of research related to organizational behavior, strategic management and sociology. The authors have utilized traditionally important work, including Lewin's ideas (1958) about the three stages of unfreeze, change and refreeze of organizations. Many others have made significant contributions (Greenwood & Hinings, 1996; Hannan & Freeman, 1984; March, 1981; Van de Ven & Poole, 1995, 2005; Weick & Quinn, 1999). A common view is that changes in organizations go from periods of revolution to longer periods of evolution.

Organizational change is often described as having two aspects—revolutionary or evolutionary. The first one could be described as a punctuated equilibrium where changes are fast and intense (Romanelli & Tushman, 1994; Tushman & Romanelli, 1985). The second one is best described as a continuous process of change (Pettigrew, 1985). Our intention is to follow some of the more radical discontinuities and rapid changes of PMOs as they frequently transform from one configuration to another. A number of studies of these types of changes have been done by Miller and Friesen (1984). This has been very successfully followed by Greenwood and Hinings (1988) with their studies of organizational archetypes or structures that create changes of patterns over time. Changes of patterns, routines and structures that occur from time to time could be constrained by inertia and are not always being recognized as full transformations (Laughlin, 1991).

Van de Ven and Poole (2005) suggested a typology of four approaches for studying organizational changes based upon the ontology and epistemology of the research. The research proposed here clearly adopts the *process study of change in organizations*: the PMO is represented as being a thing (not a verb) and is approached within both process narratives and the variance model. Adopting a process view of PMOs opens up a viewpoint on the developmental progression over time (Van de Ven, 2007).

The organizational reality in which changes occur can be quite complex, with a diversity of possible approaches. The conceptual framework of this research is developed with the intention of reflecting this diversity. Building on the discussion above and on Van de Ven and Poole (2005), this approach will be to view the changes in PMOs as a process of change with their emergent actions leading to a new PMO.

2.3.4 Drivers of Change

There are numerous drivers of organizational changes. They can be found internally and externally to organizations. Examples are: increase in complexity in external and internal environments (Ciborra, 1996), technology (Anderson & Tushman, 1990), shift in business logic (Vargo & Lusch, 2004), and integrated product and service as a unique value added solution for the customer (Brady, Davies, & Gann, 2005).

These examples could be associated with events that are outside the direct control of PMO managers. However, PMOs play an active role as participants in organizational systems. Tensions or conflicts arise around the PMO. Paraphrasing Mintzberg (1983), power in and around organizations is certainly a usual situation, giving rise to an array of different games of influence. The PMO can be identified as part of the internal structure described by analysts. Analysts are encouraged "to promote perpetual change in the organization" (p. 136). In stable periods, obviously, there is no need for analysts.

Events, political tensions and innovations create issues that lead to a need for change from the old PMO to the new PMO. Pressures from internal conflicts and politics, governmental regulations, market developments and technological changes will impact both the parent organization and the PMO, and force them to adjust themselves and to cope with these changes. External and internal triggers become drivers for change that management must address, thus forcing the organization to change and evolve.

2.4 Conceptualization of the PMO's Transformation Process

Implementing a PMO or reconfiguring an existing PMO is an important organizational change. This change is often part of a wider organizational reconfiguration. A methodology and an interpretive framework are needed to capture the dynamic complexity of organizational change. The approach that has been adopted investigates the PMO embedded in its organizational context. The approach can be related to a long tradition of contextual studies on project organizations from Midler (1994) to Pellegrinelli, Partington, Hemingway, Mohdzain, and Shah (2007). History and context are essential to the understanding of what is observed at any one point in space and time in complex systems such as organizations. The theoretical foundations of the social innovation system framework take into account the context in which such organizational innovations take place (Hughes, 1987). Social innovation also builds on a bi-directional relation that conceives of organizational innovations as socially-constructed and society-shaping (Bresnen, Goussevskaia, & Swan, 2005). Organizational innovations are produced by the interplay between actors in structures and the organization as a whole. The PMO is a socially constructed entity that in turn shapes the organization. The PMO and its host organization co-evolve with the rest of the organization.

Organizational change occurs in a political environment (Mintzberg, 1983). Changes to PMOs are caused by political forces and shape the new political environment (Donaldson, 1987). Tensions within the organization play an important role in determining the path that an organization's development will follow. In turn, each new structural arrangement realigns the power structure and creates new tensions. Thus, the investigation of the creation or restructuring of PMOs needs to integrate the political dimension of organizational change. New chief executive officer (CEO), new managers, or other changes in organization's entities may influence the development of the PMO.

This conceptual framework is process-based and aimed at capturing the PMO transformation as it unfolds. The process is embedded in the social system. The starting point is the PMO description before the transformation using the PMO model. The conditions that are associated with the transformation are then identified with external and internal drivers for change. The transformation itself is described in terms of change management. The PMO resulting from the transformation is then described using once again the PMO model. Consequences and outcomes of the change impact issues and create new issues. In this perspective, transformation of the PMO have been modeled using a framework based on conditions, action/interaction and consequences (Hobbs, Aubry, & Thuillier, 2008). These three elements form a process that repeats itself, in which consequences become the conditions for the next iteration (Strauss & Corbin, 1998). In this approach, the PMO in one period is seen as a temporary state resulting from previous conditions and generating new consequences. This sequence constitutes the basis for a PMO structuring process.

Rajagopalan and Spreitzer (1997) undertook a comprehensive review of literature on strategic change. From this review, they propose three theoretical perspectives: rational, learning or cognitive. Our research model and conceptual framework are most closely linked to the first of these, the rational perspective. In this conceptual framework, the process of PMO transformation is understood as ~~are~~ learning feedback loops. It also includes actions taken by managers as part of strategic change.

Figure 2.2 presents the conceptual framework for this research. It maintains the global process approach as proposed by Strauss and Corbin (1998) and includes the learning features proposed by Rajagopalan and Spreitzer (1997). At the beginning of the process, a PMO structure is in place. As time goes by, events happen in the environment external to the organization and become drivers for PMO change. In parallel, internal events occur and construct issues, forming the internal drivers for change.

Both external and internal drivers come from two interconnected environments. At a certain point, a decision is made by managers concerning a PMO transformation. In this framework, it is understood that managers' actions may influence their internal organization as well as their external environment. After the decision has been implemented, a new PMO structure is in place. Changes between the initial PMO structure and the structure resulting from the change may form a pattern of change. Then, the new structure produces certain outcomes in relation to the events and issues. These outcomes provide an opportunity for managers to learn from this process. Patterns refer to the scenarios of change that are found in several PMO transformations. These scenarios begin with a PMO having certain characteristics whose change is produced by specific drivers producing specific changes and impacts in the PMO. This conceptual framework is the lens through which the PMO transformation process is empirically examined.

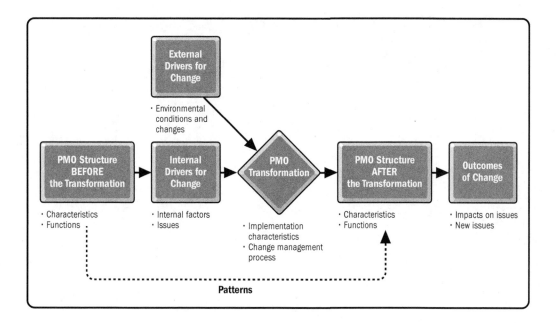

Figure 2.2. Conceptual Framework for a PMO Transformation

This chapter provided a review of the literature in three complementary fields from which the conceptual framework of the PMO's transformation process was developed. Table 2.2 presents a synthetic view of these three fields and their link to the conceptual framework.

Table 2.2. Synthetic View on Literature Review and Fit with the Conceptual Framework

Fields of the Literature Review	Major References	Conceptual Framework
1. PMO descriptive model	Hobbs & Aubry, 2010	PMO structure before the transformation PMO structure after the change
2. Organizational structure	Blomquist & Müller 2006; Burns & Stalker, 1961; Hedlund, 1994; Hobday, 2000; Mintzberg, 1989; Pettigrew, 2003	Overall framework
3. Organizational change	Burns & Stalker, 1961; Ciborra, 1996; Donaldson et al., 1996; Hughes, 1987; Massini at al., 2002; Mintzberg, 1983; Pettigrew et al., 2001	External drivers for change Internal drivers for change
	Pettigrew, 1985; Van de Ven & Poole, 2005	Patterns
	Rajagopalan & Spreitzer, 1997	PMO transformation Outcomes of change

CHAPTER THREE: METHODOLOGY

This chapter describes the underlying philosophical assumptions for this research, the research strategies and process used in the development of data collection instruments, and sampling and data collection approaches. The analysis techniques applied to the collected data are discussed in conclusion.

This specific research on PMOs in transition is part of a larger research program having already defined a global methodology approach (see the Introduction for more information on the context of the research program). In line with the global methodology, this specific research is based upon a mixed-method empirical research design which is often recognized as more robust than single methods (Brown & Eisenhardt, 1997). With the present project being part of a wider, mixed-method program of research projects, we took the epistemological perspective of realism within the present study (Bhaskar, 1975) to develop a case-based theory, following Partington (2000) in a first phase and a validation of these findings using a quantitative approach in a second phase. Realism assumes an objective reality, which can only be interpreted subjectively by human beings. To that end we assume a subjective understanding of reality, where theories are needed to allow understanding of the objective underlying mechanisms that make up the phenomenon under study.

The unit of analysis is the PMO transformation. The implementation of an organization's first PMO is a worthwhile research topic, but the context may be specific to this particular situation. For this reason, first implementations have been excluded for this research. What is of interest in this research is not the PMO entity itself, but its transformation from one state to the next. To that end, the authors began with an inductive study, using case studies to develop a questionnaire for the subsequent deductive study. This deductive study was based on a worldwide questionnaire and allowed for generally applicable results. Accordingly, the data type collected for the first study was mainly qualitative and collected via interviews and review of existing reports, whereas the data type of the second study was quantitative in order to validate results from case studies and to identify underlying structures in the PMO transformation.

Table 3.1 presents the three distinct methodological objectives for the two-phase approach. The rest of the chapter describes the phases of the research in more detail. The first section provides details from the case studies, while the second section addresses the quantitative phase of the research.

Table 3.1. Methodological Objectives by Research Phases

Phase of Research	Methodological Objectives	Time Frame
1	Investigate the present research question through use of a multi-case study approach, following Partington (2000), Eisenhardt (1989) and Yin (2003).	2008
1	Develop the data-capturing tool (i.e., a questionnaire) for the next research phase in the program by using a grounded theory approach, following Strauss and Corbin (1990).	2008
2	Validate results from case studies using the questionnaire that has been developed in the previous phase. Uncover patterns that lie beneath PMO transformations.	2008-2009

The case studies in Phase 1 were used for (a) gathering qualitative data and (b) refining the questionnaire by seeking feedback from the interviewees on the contents and layout of the survey.

3.1 Phase I: Case Studies

A case study is a comprehensive research strategy, which attempts to examine a contemporary phenomenon in its real-life context (Yin, 2003). Data was collected at two different points in time. A first set of seven cases was done in 2006 in the context of a doctoral thesis with a total of 44 interviews (Aubry, 2007). A second set of 10 cases was done early in 2008 with 29 interviews. Cases were selected to maximize the breadth of industries represented. The 17 case studies were spread over 10 different industries, with twelve of the cases in Canada and five in Sweden. Details on country, industry, number of interviews, and interviewee role are shown in Table 3.2. In total, we interviewed eleven executive managers, fifteen PMO directors, two portfolio managers, four program managers, thirteen project managers, twelve managers within PMOs, ten PMO employees and six managers elsewhere in the organization. Except for one case, sampling was done by interviewing multiple roles for each case. This approach allowed for collection of a wide spectrum of perspectives and avoided mono-source bias. Mono-method bias was minimized through the mixed-method approach in the 17 case studies and the overall research program. In line with Yin (2003), validity was pursued through careful screening and selection of possible interviewees, often involving major efforts to identify the "best" source of information. Reliability was pursued through a multi-case approach across a larger number of industries (Yin, 2003).

We used in-depth interviews during which interviewees were asked to tell us "their PMO transition story." These interviews lasted between 60 and 90 minutes. A rich data set was collected that allowed for a comprehensive understanding of the circumstances that led to the transition, the transition itself, and the implications of these transitions. For interviews done in 2006, data were recorded, transcribed and then analyzed. In 2008, data were collected through note-taking procedures.

Table 3.2. Cases and Interviewees

Transformation Cases	Country	Industry	Interviewees	
			Number of Interviews	Position
1	Canada	Telecom	2	Executive, Project Manager
2	Canada	Telecom	3	Executive, Project Manager, Manager in PMO
3	Canada	Telecom	11	Executive (2), Project Manager (3), Manager in PMO (3), PMO Director, Finances Manager, HR Manager
4	Canada	Banking	3	PMO Director, Program Manager, PMO employee
5	Canada	Banking	11	Executive, PMO Director, Portfolio Manager, Program Manager, Manager in PMO, PMO employee (3), Project Manager (2), Finances Manager
6	Canada	Home entertainment	2	PMO Director, Manager in PMO
7	Canada	Home entertainment	12	PMO Director, Manager in PMO, Project Manager, Finances Manager, HR Manager, Manager, PMO employee (6)
8	Sweden	Telecom	3	Program Manager, Portfolio Manager, PMO Director
9	Sweden	Manufacturing	3	PMO Director, Executive, Manager in PMO
10	Sweden	Defense	1	Program Manager
11	Sweden	Health Care	3	PMO Director, Manager in PMO (consultant), Executive
12	Sweden	Insurance	3	PMO Director, Project Manager, Project Manager
13	Canada	Retail	3	PMO Director, Executive (CIO), Manager in PMO (consultant)
14	Canada	Banking	3	PMO Director, Manager in PMO, Project Manager
15	Canada	Telecom-operator	3	PMO Director, Project Manager, Manager in PMO
16	Canada	Utility	3	Executive, PMO Director, Executive (Marketing unit)
17	Canada	Engineering	4	PMO Director (central), PMO Director (on client site), Project Manager, Executive (regional unit)
TOTAL			**71**	

The data from each case were used for within-case analyses, done by the interviewing researchers immediately after the interviews. This analysis step aimed at building a cohesive story of the context, the PMO itself and its transition. Evidence beyond the interview data was taken from reports, the questionnaire, and other material, including organizational charts and internal presentations given to the team during the interview. The results were summarized in case reports, which, along with interview notes, were used for the cross-case analysis after all interviews had been completed. The questionnaire played a major role in the 10 interviews conducted in 2008 (see Appendix B for the questionnaire):

- Each interviewee received a copy of the questionnaire prior to the interview, and was encouraged to complete it prior to the interview. Approximately 80% of the interviewees did so.

- During the second part of the interview we talked through the questionnaire question-by-question to better understand their answers and to seek feedback on how to refine the questionnaire.
- After the interview, we analyzed the answers, refined the questionnaire and revised questions for the next interview. The results of the analysis led to an immediate update of the questionnaire.

The questionnaire was developed through a three-step process during the qualitative phase of the research. The first version was piloted in Sweden and then revised into a second version, which was then piloted in Canada. New comments from Canadian interviewees lead to a third version of the questionnaire that was used in the next phase of the research.

The cross-case analyses focused on the identification of demographic, external, internal, procedural, and performance conditions or drivers of change. This was done jointly by all researchers through a constant comparison approach, following Strauss and Corbin (1990). For this we compared the within-case analyses and the associated interview notes to derive 33 cross-case drivers that describe the context, scope and nature of the transition of the PMOs. Then we defined these 33 drivers in detail, using the interview notes, questionnaire responses and a variety of published academic sources. A distinction was made between drivers that were events in context of the PMO and tensions or issues that arose in the organization, which led to a change in the PMO. (A tension or an issue is, for these purposes, defined as a subject of discussion and debate.) A further distinction was made between events internal to the organization and events external to the organization. The drivers and their definitions can be found in Appendix C.

The next step in data analysis was to identify the weight of each of the 33 drivers. We used contents analysis in the form of the relative frequency of references to the different drivers to identify their importance (Denzin & Lincoln, 2000). In the final step, the drivers mentioned most often were clustered by their logical relationships, in order to identify the main clusters of drivers in PMO transitions. Details of the analysis are reported in Chapter Five.

3.2 Phase II: The Survey

As described in the previous section, the survey questionnaire was developed, tested and refined in Phase I.

3.2.1 Data Collection Strategy

As explained in the precedent section, the questionnaire has been pilot-tested during the qualitative phase of this research in Sweden and in Canada. The resulting questionnaire, including the enhancements from the pilot tests, has been pre-tested with ten new respondents in both languages, French and English. Very few modifications came out from this test. Then, the web-based questionnaire was launched.

Items in the questionnaire reflect the basic constructs from the conceptual framework (see Figure 2.3). Appendix D presents the alignment between these constructs and the questionnaire. Internal and external drivers were assessed on a nine-point scale from one being unimportant to nine being very important. PMO structure before and after the PMO transformation refers to almost the same set of questions, which describe the structural characteristics (13 questions) and functions (two questions) at two different points in time, i.e., ex-ante and ex-post the transition of the PMO. Similar nine-point scales were used, except in cases where numbers or percentages were required. The construct for PMO transformation used similar scales to assess time and magnitude of the transformation and the change process (four questions). The outcome construct mirrors the issues that were proposed as internal drivers for change. It answers the question of whether the PMO transformation has impact on the original issue that led to the change.

We applied non-probability sampling using a snowball approach to professionals, professional organizations, and researchers. While this approach does not allow for the calculation of a traditional response rate, it does ensure quality in the answers, as only members of professional organizations or personal networks with known levels of expertise were targeted.

The questionnaire was distributed to:

- Personal contacts of the researchers
- Local communities of practices or interest groups on PMOs or related themes
- International interest groups on PMOs
- PMI local chapters
- Events within the project management community
- LinkedIn and Facebook groups on project management and PMOs
- PMI web site

After a first invitation to answer the survey, two reminders were sent in two- to three-week intervals. The number of valid responses was 184, sufficient for the statistical analyses we had planned.

Validity of the data was addressed through various means. Validity ensures that a measurement tool (such as a questionnaire) measures what it is supposed to measure. Validity of the data was ensured through the comprehensive questionnaire development and piloting process explained above. Concept, construct and face validity were addressed through this approach. Moreover, by targeting a sampling frame of project management professionals from professional organizations, and the authors' personal networks with known levels of professionalism, valid answers which are representative of professional project managers were assured.

3.2.2 Data Analysis Strategy

Three levels of statistical analysis were undertaken:
- Descriptive
- Factor analysis and correlation analysis
- Multi-variate regression analysis and moderated hierarchical regression analysis

Descriptive analysis aims at presenting an overall view on the data; results are presented in details in Chapter Six. Chapter Seven presents the results from factor and correlation analysis and Chapter Eight presents the results from the moderated hierarchical regression analyses.

Factor analysis. The survey aims at providing a better understanding of (1) the conditions that lead to changes in PMOs, (2) the nature of the changes to the PMOs and (3) the importance of the impacts of these changes.

Accordingly, three groups of variables were formed. Each of these groups contains many variables. Factor analysis using principal component analysis and a Varimax rotation was used to identify the underlying psychological structures of each of these groups' respondents and to reduce the number of variables. The objective was to reduce the variables to the smallest number of unique elements that can be considered to make up the phenomenon under study.

Four different factor analyses were undertaken. The first two analyses addressed conditions leading to changes in PMOs; these are first, the internal and external events, and secondly, the issues related to PMO change. The resulting factors were:
1. Event factors
2. Issue factors

The third factor analysis addressed the changes to the PMOs, which are the differences between the characteristics of the PMOs before and after the change. The fourth factor analysis addressed the impacts achieved after the PMO transition. That led to factors:
3. PMO change factors
4. Impact factors

Reliability of the factor data was tested using Cronbach Alpha. Factors with alpha values above 0.6 were considered reliable (Cronbach, 1951). Factor loadings above 0.5 were considered significant (Hair, Anderson, Tatham, & Black, 1998). Those factors that did not meet these two threshold levels were considered orphans and listed in the respective tables, but excluded from further analyses. The details of the method are described at the beginning of Chapter Seven.

Correlation analysis. In order to identify possible patterns in the change process, correlation analyses were performed first among the factors identified and between the factors and several contextual variables. Both the details of the method employed and the results are presented in Chapter Seven.

Multi-variate regression and mediating and moderating effects. A series of hierarchical regression analyses were performed to test for the moderating effects mentioned above. That means an assessment was done on:

- Whether a variable qualified as a moderator
- The potential impact a hypothesized mediating and/or moderating variable has on the nature and the strength of the relationships between the independent and dependent variables.

Three groups of variables were identified:

1. Independent variable (event and issue factors), to summarize the events and the issues that drive or trigger the transition of PMOs
2. Dependent variables (impact factors), to summarize the impact the transition had on the PMO
3. Mediating and moderating variables (PMO change factors and individual contextual variables), to summarize the changes to the PMO that were made through the transition, plus to take into consideration the context within which the transitions took place.

Details on these statistical analyses are presented in Chapter Eight. Overall, this chapter described the underlying assumptions, the process and the analysis techniques used for the study. The next chapters will describe the results of the analysis following the global methodology strategy: description of case studies in Chapter Four, results from case studies in Chapter Five, and results from the survey in Chapters Six, Seven and Eight.

CHAPTER FOUR: DESCRIPTION OF CASE STUDIES

As presented in the chapter on methodology, case studies were initiated first with the goal of capturing the essential PMO transformations that would eventually lead to the construction of a large-scale questionnaire for the second phase of this research. In the following section, descriptions of the 17 case studies are presented. See Table 4.1 for a complete list of the case studies. Fictitious names have been given to organizations to save their confidentiality. The level of analysis within this research is the PMO transformation. As can be observed from Table 4.1, in some organizations multiple transformations were documented either as successive distinct configurations of the same PMO or of different PMOs within the same organization.

Table 4.1. List of Case Studies by Organization and Industrial Sector

Organization Number	Organization Name	Industrial Sector	Case Study Number of Transformations	
1	The Network Company	Telecommunications	3	#1, #2, #3
2	The Bank	Financial - Banking	2	#4, #5
3	The Gamer	Home Entertainment	2	#6, #7
4	The Developer Company	Telecommunications	1	#8
5	The Pack	Manufacturer	1	#9
6	The Armour	Security and Defense	1	#10
7	The Hospital	Health - Public	1	#11
8	The Data Warehouse	Financial - Insurance	1	#12
9	The Store	Sales - Retailing	1	#13
10	The Financial Group	Financial - Banking	1	#14
11	The Telephone Company	Telecommunications – Operator	1	#15
12	The Power Company	Facilities - Public	1	#16
13	The Engineering Company	Engineering	1	#17
TOTAL			**17**	

The description of each case study follows the same format in two parts: first, the organizational context is presented, followed by the description of the PMO transformation (multiple descriptions are given when appropriate). Each section ends with a synthetic view of each transformation presented in a short table based upon the major elements from the conceptual framework (see Figure 2.2).

4.1 Organization 1: "The Network Company"

4.1.1 Organizational Context

"The Network Company," over 50 years old, was a leading company in telecommunications equipment for both hardware and software systems. The focus of this research was on a local R&D center, hereafter "The R&D Center." The telecommunication industry was recognized as growing and fast pace changing since the 90s. Many new technologies in the voice and image transmission and Internet facilities have enhanced the internal capabilities of the whole industry, moving from hardware engineering systems to software systems and finally to multiple types of message integration.

The Network Company has known an unprecedented growth during the 1990s, followed by the fall of the market in 2001 and then a cautious rise since 2004. Technology and economic changes have repercussions inside the organization. The word "reorganization" came back in a recurrent form in the responses to the survey, and innovation was a major issue in this context. This company invested heavily in R&D and maintained its strategy of investment, even during the dark period from 2001 to 2004.

4.1.2 First Transformation of the PMO

The first transformation of the PMO referred to the step between the first PMO and the following stage. The first PMO in The R&D Center was implemented in 1992. The head office also adopted a delocalization strategy concerning their R&D centers that was believed to stimulate innovation. Consequently, the business relationship with the client became the direct responsibility of the PMO and the overall responsibilities became larger and more strategic. The PMO was centralized and made responsible for business results. Only a restricted portion of project managers were included in it (see Table 4.2).

This strategy gave such good results that The R&D Center became an important entity with great visibility in the market. However, The R&D Center's success also created tensions with the head office, which took umbrage at this situation. The head office was afraid to be perceived as a having a secondary role in front of their customers, as noted by a manager: "I thought that [The R&D Center] had a lot more exposure to the market, a lot more than what was happening there [in the head office] […] where I think it was a bit more the back office."

In an exponentially growing international market, the head office changed its delocalization strategy to a centralized approach based upon the desire to serve their major customers through a unique entry to the overall organization. This change has led to an overall restructuration in 1996 that affected all entities of the company including The R&D Center.

Consequently, the responsibility for client relationships was transferred back to the head office, which once more handled business aspects of projects. However, industry was still in a rapid growth period and multiple new developments were entrusted to The R&D Center; thus, The R&D Center's responsibilities were focused on technology that was changing rapidly with increasing levels of complexity. On the heels of The R&D Center's restructuring, the PMO remained centralized and took a more technical role. Even if this PMO lost the responsibility to build client relationships, it became more powerful, and for the first time, project managers were a part of that change.

Table 4.2. The Network Company: First PMO Transformation

		PMO TRANSFORMATION #1
Conditions	External drivers	Perception of endless growth in the industry
		Technological innovations in voice and image transmission
	Internal drivers	Exponential growth in this R&D center (number of projects and number of employees)
		Strategy in R&D: centralization of decisions and relationship with customers
		Aligned with the global restructuration of the company
	Issues	The transformation corresponds to the loss of the "business" side of projects, including the relationship with customers, which was centralized.
		Centered on "technical" project management. Project managers mostly came from internal, technical departments of the organization.
PMO Before	Structural characteristics	Unique centralized PMO
		PM partly within PMO
	Most important functions	Customer Interface
The Transformation	Difficulty of implementation	No major problems in PMO implementation
PMO After	Structural characteristics	Unique centralized PMO
		PM all within PMO
	Most important functions	Monitoring of project performance
		Competencies in PM
Consequences	Impact in issues	Development of strong technical skills for project managers
	New issues	PMO put emphasis toward technical part of projects, neglecting the "management" part

4.1.3 Second Transformation of the PMO

The second transformation happened in 1998, after a two-year period with the precedent PMO. At that time, growth in the global telecommunications market was still on the rise. At the head office level as well as in The R&D Center, a business unit structure was adopted. Four business units were put in place in The R&D Center, each one adopting its own PMO structure. The centralized PMO had been dismantled in order to give a sense of small enterprises to each of the business units. These business units were only responsible for the technology development of projects.

An important fact to mention is that this structure was relatively stable until 2004, a few years after the bubble burst of 2001. There was major turbulence in this industry from 2001 to 2004, but The R&D Center was spared and the PMO structure remained almost unchanged (see Table 4.3).

Tensions at play during this second transformation were related to the desire of the executive team to gain autonomy in the way they managed their projects. The perception from the executive team was that the technical orientation taken by the PMO was not flexible enough to create new products for customers. The PMO didn't match the company's need for innovation and creativity within a growing telecommunication market. As a result, flexibility was strongly encouraged in this transformation of The R&D Center. In 1998, The R&D Center was restructured into four business units to create something similar to a "small company approach." The four PMOs were slightly different in their scope and mission, answering the specific needs of their assigned business unit. Generally, they were oriented to provide support for projects driven by business units needs. The global result was redundancy in methodology, processes and tools, with each PMO arguing its uniqueness and specificity.

Table 4.3. The Network Company: Second PMO Transformation

		PMO TRANSFORMATION #2
Conditions	External drivers	Perception of endless growth in the industry
		Technological innovations in voice and image transmission
	Internal drivers	Projects are more complex: technology, management and customers
		Search for innovativeness
	Issues	Centralized PMO prevents innovation and creativity
PMO Before	Structural characteristics	Unique centralized PMO: project management all within PMO
	Most important functions	Monitoring of project performance
		Competencies in project management
The Transformation	Difficulty of implementation	
PMO After	Structural characteristics	Multiple PMOs, each one in a business unit, including project management
	Most important functions	Methodology, processes and tools
Consequences	Impact in issues	
	New issues	Increase in the costs of PMO
		Problem with delivery dates
		Multiple entry points for customer, which created confusion

4.1.4 Third Transformation of the PMO

In 2001, the technology bubble burst, creating a difficult period for this company and more generally for the industry. This company maintained its long-term development perspective and long-term R&D objectives while cutting into the operations side of the business. Because of this strategy, the economic downturn had few consequences in the short term for The R&D Center (see Table 4.4).

The third transformation happened in 2004 within a global restructuring. At that time, the global financial results of the company were encouraging after a three-year period of difficulties. But the organizational efficiency program was still focused on R&D activities, after having optimized the operations side of the business. The organizational efficiency program led to reshaping The R&D Center globally, and for the first time in this center, layoffs occurred.

The R&D Center had to prove its capacity to compete with the other centers. Other R&D centers had been put in place over the past few years, particularly in emerging countries where human resource costs were cheaper than in the western countries. Internal competition existed and the decision to make a center responsible for a project was based largely on human resource costs.

Moreover, quality in project management deteriorated significantly during the precedent PMO period. "He [head of The R&D Center] came into a unit that was responsible of 60% of the delays […] and had a very bad reputation]," mentioned the new PMO director of the previous director. This result was visible in the annual report where statistics were presented specifically on this indicator of respect of the delivery date. These drivers led to profound changes in the way of managing projects.

The new CEO and his management team proceeded as follows during the reorganization: diagnostic firsts, followed by solutions and actions. "We established [a] centralized project office with a very specific purpose. So we didn't establish the project office by deciding to go centralize and then moving forward with the project office. It was the other way around," stated the PMO director.

It resulted in a strong centralization movement accompanied by a strict control over the projects. Business units remained in place but project management was completely centralized. The project managers returned to the centralized and unique PMO. They were assigned to the projects of a business unit as consultants. The resulting structure brought two-sided management styles: one side looking after business benefits while the other side was looking after the project processes results.

This way of managing projects required cooperation between the business managers and the project managers. The first major issue to become apparent was the need for transparency. It became very difficult to hide unpleasant information. This aspect was linked to the issue of equilibrium between the search for quality of the product and the search for quality of project. This tension could be a positive one, but it required discussion and dialogue between business and project managers.

The profile of project managers also changed. Instead of their previous technical role, project managers were now asked to be true managers and leaders. An executive at the R&D Center said that this was "because project management is all about leadership…and this means that the project manager should be the leader, the CEO of that small organization." Project managers who didn't meet these qualifications were asked to resign while others were trained as leaders.

Table 4.4. The Network Company: Third PMO Transformation

		PMO TRANSFORMATION #3
Conditions	External drivers	Fragility of the industry
	Internal drivers	Customer-centered strategy
		Internal competition between R&D centers
	Issues	Centralized PMO prevents innovation and creativity
PMO Before	Structural characteristics	Unique centralized PMO: project management all within PMO
	Most important functions	Monitor project performance
		Competencies
The Transformation	Difficulty of implementation	Great difficulties in implementation of the new PMO
PMO After	Structural characteristics	Multiple PMOs, each one in a business unit, including project management
	Most important functions	Methodology, processes, and tools
Consequences	Impact in issues	Control of project costs and delivery dates
	New issues	Project manager profiles of those who remained and those who were laid off
		Transparency in information
		Tension between quality of product and respect of delivery date

4.2 Organization 2: "The Bank"

4.2.1 Organizational Context

"The Bank" was a hundred-year old financial institution which showed good economic indicators between 2000 and 2005, as did most banks in the western world. This industry was service-driven, and projects were realized for internal customers. The financial industry went through a quasi-revolution in the 1980s with deregulation, technological innovations, globalization of markets and new non brick-and-mortar competitors (Roberts & Amit, 2003). This profound transformation was brought about by major innovation in information technology (software and hardware) and telecommunications. Since then, the number of projects increased at a steady pace, and most of those projects had a strong IT component.

The two transformations of the PMO presented in the following cover a period of 10 years, with a first PMO implementation in 1996. During that period, revenues of The Bank grew by almost 50%, while at the same time the number of employees went down, showing a loss of 30% in 2003 before regaining 20%

by 2005. Adding to a net loss in terms of number of employees, the type of work significantly changed over the same period, from a more operational workload to an information-based workload.

4.2.2 First Transformation of the PMO

In 1996, the first PMO was put in place when the company initiated the large Re-Engineering Project, the largest project they had ever undertaken at a budget of over 500 million dollars. The re-engineering effort was motivated by the threat from international agencies to decrease the risk quotation, which would have had a dramatic impact on the overall organization. At that time, the operational costs were the highest in the country. The Re-Engineering Project completely changed the way services were delivered to customers. Business solutions based upon an IT virtual distribution chain (such as Internet, automatic teller, etc.) were implemented.

From an organizational perspective, business managers wanted control over decision-making processes, as that control had been transferred to IT departments for many years. Changes in decision-making processes led to the creation of a specific structure for the Re-Engineering Project. This structure integrated the expertise required for the development of sub-projects under the Re-Engineering Project, resulting in a matrix structure for the first time in the organizational history of The Bank. The PMO was located at the top level within the Re-Engineering Project. It included all project managers, most of them being consultants. This period gave rise to a project management culture. This PMO lasted for almost five years without major changes.

However, dissatisfaction began during this stage with a lack of expected outcomes and reduction in operational costs, which was the raison-d'être of this initiative. This phenomenon was common to many re-engineering projects undertaken at that time. Tensions and conflicts arose over two years, leading to the layoffs of almost every management member of the Re-Engineering Project team. Without convincing results that lowered operational costs, the organization was still pressured by international agencies to find other solutions.

In 2001, the company proceeded with the merger of 11 autonomous regional units within the head office. These mergers kept operational costs at the lowest possible level in a very competitive market. The Enterprise PMO arose from the awareness that a global view of all the projects of the organization was missing, as was a view of the overall development of the company. For the first time ever, projects and strategy were under the same roof. The matrix structure was reinforced and project managers were confirmed in their positions as PMO employees. It was during this period that the concept of a portfolio of projects emerged and a Project Priority Board (PPB) was created to enable the Board of Directors to concentrate on its operational business role without being directly involved in the projects.

However, the legitimacy of the PMO was questioned during this period. Executives declared that they were only willing to be fully accountable for project results if they were allowed to fully manage them. Despite these issues, the PMO lasted for almost five years, until it became obvious that the PMO's survival depended on a major change in its mission. Fortunately, business objectives (in terms of operational costs) had been met, and pressures were relaxed. This caused a change in the strategy of The Bank, which refocused efforts on development versus cost control. See Table 4.5.

Table 4.5. The Bank: First PMO Transformation

		PMO TRANSFORMATION #4
Conditions	External drivers	Pressure from international agencies to decrease to risk quotation
		Revolution in the financial industry
		Deregulation and entry of new international competitors
	Internal drivers	Global restructuring to decrease operational costs
		Change in the executive team and in the PMO
	Issues	Lack of results on operational costs from Re-Engineering Project
		Tension between people working inside the project versus those working outside the project
PMO Before	Structural characteristics	Unique central PMO dedicated to Re-Engineering Projects
		51-100 projects
		100% projects of this part of organization
		90% of project management
		10-12 employees in the PMO
		Moderate level of authority
		100% control over the resources (less matrix)
	Most important functions	Monitor project performance
		Customer interface
The Transformation	Difficulty of implementation	Uneasy PMO implementation in relation to cultural change of project management
PMO After	Structural characteristics	Unique central Enterprise PMO with governance committee
		101-500 projects
		80% of projects of organization
		Nine employees in the PMO
		Little authority
		Less than 20% of resources under its control (very matrix)
	Most important functions	Customer interface
Consequences	Impact on issues	No legitimacy for the PMO: maintained as an insurance policy, requiring regular justification for PMO survival
		Objectives reached in terms of decreasing operational costs
	New issues	Accountability for project: manager from business side (versus desire for project managers within unit)
		PMO responsible for the project budget envelope (tension)
		Major programs that failed in part because of a lack of cooperation between units

Similar situation (A) to BMS 2018 (handwritten)

4.2.3 Second Transformation of the PMO

The implementation of the new strategy for business development took place in 2004 with a major restructuring based on a business unit approach. Each business unit was given the full accountability to reach their specific business objectives, including the management and implementation of their projects. Consequently, the role of the Enterprise PMO from the previous period had now been spread among multiple units, most of which were not called PMOs. Project managers were moved to these business units. This way of spreading multiple project management entities can be compared with *balkanization,* or division and compartmentalization (Merriam-Webster, 2007).

A central PMO was left at the top level. This PMO was responsible for strategy, control and support and it was focused on three major elements: to advise the PPB, to ensure the control of all projects in the organization, and to support project managers throughout the organization with a standard methodology. The business units were then reinforced and redefined as accountable for the results of their project portfolios, including benefits. Project managers were grouped within PMOs in different business units. Their role was to execute projects as planned and to control their scope, schedule and costs. Having been assigned the role of controlling projects, the business unit PMO was now at a comparable position to the central PMO. This situation led to tensions and conflicts on the interpretation of the real status of projects (see Table 4.6).

Table 4.6. The Bank: Second PMO Transformation

		PMO TRANSFORMATION #5
Conditions	External drivers	Banks making huge profits – population reacts negatively
	Internal drivers	New strategy: business development
		Major restructuring: business units
		New management team
	Issues	No legitimacy for the PMO: maintained as an insurance policy, requiring regular justification for PMO survival
		Accountability for project: manager from business side buy out. They want project managers in their own unit.
		The PMO, responsible for the project budget envelope (tension)
		Problem with three major programs that failed in part because of a lack of cooperation between units
PMO Before	Structural characteristics	Unique central Enterprise PMO with governance committee
		101-500 projects
		80% of projects of the whole organization
		Nine employees in the PMO
		Little level of authority
		Less than 20% over the resources (very matrix)
	Most important functions	Customer Interface
The Transformation	Difficulty of implementation	Very difficult
PMO After	Structural characteristics	Central
		51-100 projects
		100% of projects within the organization
		No project manager
		Fourteen employees in the PMO
		Almost no authority over projects
		0% of resources working in projects, under the control of the PMO manager.
	Most important functions	Monitor project performance
		Methodology, standards & tools
Consequences	Impact in issues	Accountability for projects clearly established to be under BU
	New issues	PMO wants to control the "project machine" through alignment with strategy
		Process versus business struggles within the Project Governance Board
		Difficulties reinforcing relationship with project's customers
		Perceived loss of synergy between project managers

4.3 Organization 3: "The Gamer"

4.3.1 Organizational Context

"The Gamer" was a producer of home entertainment products. The company was originally a family enterprise that went public after ten years. It was part of a new technology sector and was expanding very rapidly, especially in technical software and hardware innovations. This sector was then, and still is, devoted to procuring pleasure for its customers. "The Gamer's" internal philosophy was based on developing strong internal development capabilities, rather than adopting a niche strategy. The focus of this case study was the largest development center of the company. Projects required a significant number of resources. In the peak period of a project, over 200 persons may have worked in parallel.

The local development center was created in the mid-1990s and quickly became the most important development center outside the head office country. The head office kept all strategic issues as its own responsibility and left execution to the local center. The local center was organized functionally, with each project managed by one function and the components of the project sequentially completed one function after the other. This center was asked to increase the number of projects and to accelerate the rhythm of delivery. The functional structure struggled to meet these new requirements.

In 2000, a new executive was appointed as the local center CEO and saw in the project-based organization the opportunity to contribute to the growth expectations. Projects became the base of this new form of organizing, despite the fact that some general functions remained at the global level (for instance, human resources and finance). The first PMO was put in place with a focus on planning issues, in order to coordinate activities and resources for rapid delivery. The first PMO director, despite being hired for skills in project management and performance, did not meet company expectations of accelerated project deliveries. A new PMO director was hired and this led to the first PMO transformation.

4.3.2 First Transformation of the PMO

In 2003, industry growth was still persistent. The technology infrastructure was gaining in complexity with the arrival of new platforms that did not displace older platforms. However, the industry was still driven by the time-to-market constraint, and it was more difficult to keep the tempo of accelerating project deliveries in this context. With a new PMO director, approaches and processes were drastically changed to increase productivity. Strict processes were abandoned and flexibility in planning tools was permitted, which allowed workers to use a variety of software. Despite the flexibility in planning tools, the new PMO director strictly required that project managers provide the exact resource utilization ratio for their project on a regular basis. Based on each project ratio, the PMO director was able to prepare the global resource utilization report for the company and to plan for future needs and availability for new projects, both being very strategic for the company (see Table 4.7).

Table 4.7. The Gamer: First PMO Transformation

		PMO TRANSFORMATION #6
Conditions	External drivers	Growth in the video game industry and simultaneous aggressive competition
	Internal drivers	Strategy of vertical integration instead of niche strategy
		Important problems with allocation of resources
		CEO and management team change: following structure of project-oriented organization
		Need to augment production considerably
	Issues	Parent organization wants to control local center
		Recent entry to public market
		Complexity in projects due to variety of technological platforms
		Internal struggle over what was perceived as excessive rigor in planning
PMO Before	Structural characteristics	One central agency in a functional unit
		Very few projects
		All projects
		0% of project manager
		One employee in PMO
		Little decision-making authority
		Very matrix (0% of people on projects under the control of PMO's director)
	Most important functions	Methodology, standards and tools
The Transformation	Difficulty of implementation	Difficult PMO implementation due to strict rigor in specific project management ratio
PMO After	Structural characteristics	Less than 10 projects
		Four employees in PMO
	Most important functions	Monitor and control project performance
		Methodology, standards and tools
		Competencies in project management
		Multi-project management
		Strategic management
		Organizational knowledge
		HR
		Specialized tasks
Consequences	Impact in issues	No change in the relation with the parent organization: still in conflict
		Working by program eases management of platform
		Tensions related to rigor on planning relaxed
	New issues	Producers worried about the control of project: fragile equilibrium
		Commercialization strategy developed far from targeted market

4.3.3 Second Transformation of the PMO

Industry continued to grow. In 2005, complexity related to the variety of the technology continued to increase, augmenting the pressure on project teams to deliver on time. This period of the PMO's evolution was in continuity with the previous one; there was no new PMO director and no change in the PMO's scope. Program management was added to the mandate of the PMO in order to better coordinate multiple projects. Project managers were grouped by program. The PMO mirrored this change by adding a program management level in its structure (see Table 4.8).

Table 4.8. The Gamer: Second PMO Transformation

		PMO TRANSFORMATION #7
Conditions	External drivers	Growth in the video game industry; competition even more aggressive in this market
		Important grants available from government
		Constant evolution of technology with new features, enhanced player experience and new platform
		Customer demand for heightened experience in product
	Internal drivers	Maintenance of strategy of vertical integration instead of niche strategy
		Need to augment production considerably
		Internal competition from other local development center
	Issues	Desire for control by parent organization
		Complexity in projects due to variety of technological platforms
		Struggles between producer (actual PM) and PMO where project coordinators are located
		PMO blamed for not acting when necessary
		Internal struggles due to employees' perception of overly rigorous planning requirements (what was perceived as to much rigor in planning)
		Standardization not encouraged: each team has its own tools and process
		Quality of product was questioned
PMO Before	Structural characteristics	One central agency in a functional unit
		Very few projects (2-3)
		All projects
		0% of project manager
		One employee in PMO
		Little decision-making
		Very matrix (0% of people on projects under the control of PMO's director)
	Most important functions	Monitor and control project performance
		Methodology, standards and tools
		Competencies in project management
		Multi-project management
		Strategic management
		Organizational knowledge
		HR
		Specialized tasks
The Transformation	Difficulty of implementation	Easy
PMO After	Structural characteristics	More: 11-50 projects
		Adding a layer for program management
	Most important functions	Monitor and control project performance
		Methodology, standards and tools
		Competencies in project management
		Multi-project management
		Strategic management
		Organizational knowledge
		HR
Consequences	Impact on issues	PMO receives criticism for lack of action when project fails
	New issues	Increase in tensions between local center and the head office

4.4 Organization 4: "The Developer"

4.4.1 Organizational Context

"The Developer" was a business unit at "SystemsCorp," a firm integrating software and hardware in a product delivered and sold to global customers. For the last few years, The Developer had been working with multimedia applications. SystemsCorp was always aware of competitors and their moves, as well as potential customers. The company was also well aware that in a highly competitive marketplace, not being a first player in the market could make a big difference in revenue and market share. To be on the edge was, and may still be, a way of life in this industry. The Developer had about 2,000 employees in several locations. See Table 4.9.

4.4.2 Transformation of the PMO

SystemsCorp had a history of creating structures and procedures around projects. This included an array of structures for governing individual projects and working with project portfolios and programs. Prior to 2004, the PMO at The Developer was organized to manage a group of development programs. Each program had its own program manager responsible for ongoing projects.

The PMO supported the different program managers in their undertakings and organized integration with other corporate business systems for reporting on the performance of different products. Even with an effectively-designed project governance structure, The Developer found that it needed to speed up its response to adjust to market changes and market demands. This led to the PMO transformation.

A new chief information officer (CIO) for the business unit and a new PMO manager came to The Developer. Both were internal promotions and had received guidance about faster delivery times and flexibility. The transformation then shifted from a project and program view to a product and program view. The product life cycle was seen as essential and old program managers needed to become product managers to remain successful. The whole R&D process changed from larger projects to smaller projects, often with only 10-12 persons involved (instead of hundreds). There were stage gates throughout the old project management procedures, and changes to a series of product decisions as to whether to continue developing the current product or terminate it. This made it possible to make late changes in the development of a product. A second possibility with this approach was a better ability to work more on the road map of products instead of on large inflexible projects. Company's executives decided that too much time and effort had been put into making requests for changes while handing over projects from one stage to another.

Table 4.9. The Developer: PMO Transformation

		PMO TRANSFORMATION #8
Conditions	External drivers	Increasing demand to respond to customer and market
	Internal drivers	New CEO and PMO
	Issues	Too much time spent on changes
		Too much time spent on handing over projects between stages
PMO Before	Structural characteristics	PMO part of the business unit
		Project managers within the PMO
		Traditional project management methodology
	Most important functions	Project management
The Transformation	Difficulty of implementation	Duration of transformation and depth of change
PMO After	Structural characteristics	Within a business unit
		Projects much smaller in size and scope
		From project life cycle to product life cycle
	Most important functions	Program management
		Experimentation of Agile project management methodology to reduce response time for changes
Consequences	Impact on issues	Delivering usable and valuable results in a frequent and structured way
	New issues	Issues with project managers becoming program managers

4.5 Organization 5: "The Pack"

4.5.1 Organizational Context

"The Pack" was a family owned company that has been in business for more than 50 years. It was a manufacturer of packages for liquid food. Traditionally, its market was based in Europe. By 2005, sales reached their limit and resulted in a stable situation while the context of the packaging industry itself evolved into an intense phase of consolidation. On the one hand, the competition became more intense, even fierce, while on the other hand new opportunities in developing countries began to appear with rapid improvement in the purchasing power of the middle class. This led in 2006 to a new three-fold strategy:

- Focus on and grow the core
- Emphasize cost-driven innovation
- Drive operational performance

These changes in the strategy took place in a "new organization" where employees and units needed to work together more effectively. Where it had been a business unit structure, the organization returned to what can be described as a functionalistic structure with a more centralized decision-making process. Employees were also involved in the implementation of the strategy with a specific capabilities strategy. Project management was recognized as an essential capability needed to reach the strategic objectives.

4.5.2 Transformation of the PMO

The global reorganization entailed a transformation of the project structures. The transformation referred to the passage from one PMO within a business unit to a PMO within the R&D unit of the functional organization. In both situations, multiple PMOs existed in the organization.

The first PMO was implemented in 2004, within a particular Business Unit (BU) dedicated to R&D projects and located outside the head office country. This BU was the most important for the company. At that time, the PMO's primary focus was placed on processes and tasks, leaving competencies and training in project management as a second priority.

Given the importance of this BU, the company was sensitive to any variation in sales and revenues from it. The first driver for change was associated with failures of two major projects causing major losses. This issue, in addition to others from economic and industrial contexts, led to the global reorganization of the company.

New upper managers came into the organization and, with them, new values and a new management philosophy. As mentioned by a manager within the organization, the "new boss" moved away from an "obsession with rules, procedures, and processes." Seen from this view, the PMO became a business enabler instead of a policeman.

The fault with these project failures was associated with a lack in project management competencies. More than that, as the market changed, it was necessary for the project management to adapt to a multicultural context. Training had been adjusted to face this new situation.

After the transformation, this PMO was responsible for R&D projects within the global organization. Project managers were not included in the PMO, as was the case before. Even if the number of projects remained almost the same, the scope of this new PMO was larger in relation to projects of the organization. The PMO split into two locations in two different countries. Half of the staff of the PMO was located at the head office while the other half operated in a business unit outside the country. The director of the PMO was located within the business unit and visited the head office once per month.

Focus on people. Under the leadership of the new boss and with an awareness of the lack of competencies in project management, the focus of the PMO directly addressed the development of capabilities in project management. The PMO was redefined as a center of excellence that sought to deliver value, not rules and processes. The development of competencies was achieved through a model of role awareness that help project managers to assess their position within this model and to develop themselves along a career path. This model was broader than traditional training in project management such as certification given from PMI, APMI or Prince2. In this model, training was not sufficient for developing the role awareness; employees required mentoring and networking. PMI certification was encouraged but was complemented by an internal certification in project management. This focus on people was reflected in an increase in the importance of the functions of competencies in project management, organizational learning and HR.

The PMO as participant in the business decision-making process. The director of the PMO participated in the governance board of the company. He provided information for decision-making in relation to projects. In this regard, the PMO developed portfolio management.

Organizational commitment to project management. Members of the Board acknowledged project management competency as an essential capability for company health. This represented a change from the previous organizational culture. At the same time, competencies of project managers were being developed. Notably, a gap still existed between project managers and the Board. Middle managers were not recognized as stakeholders in this change. Executives were convinced that more work needed to be done in order to gain their complete support for the project management culture. As mentioned by a PMO manager: "The word *project* is not understood in the same way by the financial controllers and the owners." See Table 4.10.

Table 4.10. The Pack: PMO Transformation

		PMO TRANSFORMATION #9
Conditions	External drivers	Developing countries: "growing markets are now in India, China and Russia"
		Fierce competition in packaging market
	Internal drivers	Stasis of growth: develop a new strategy and reorganization
		New CEO
		Project failures due in part to lack of competencies in PM
	Issues	Too many rules and standards
		PMO as police
PMO Before	Structural characteristics	Within Business Unit
	Most important functions	Monitor project performance
		Methodology, standards and tools
The Transformation	Difficulty of implementation	Somewhat easy
PMO After	Structural characteristics	Within functional unit
		Greater % of projects in organization
		Larger staff in PMO
		Larger decision-making authority
		Larger accountability for project results
	Most important functions	Competencies in project management
		Organizational learning
		HR
Consequences	Impact on issues	Focus on people: seen as a key for success in project
		Better credibility of PMO: participation on the Board
	New issues	A gap exists between upper management and project managers: "the word project is not understood in the same way by the financial controller and the owners"

4.6 Organization 6: "The Armour"

4.6.1 Organizational Context

"The Armour" was a developer and producer of high-tech security goods. It had a clear niche with core knowledge used in the development of advanced solutions for civil and military systems that can be airborne, ground-based or naval. The Armour employed 1,500 employees and was a subsidiary firm within a larger group of advanced system products. Products were developed and manufactured in close relation to the end user. Today, customers for companies of this nature are found in a global market. The change in the market transitioned the firm from a few local customers to a group of international customers.

In 2005, The Armour was purchased by the owner of a firm with which it had a working relationship for many decades. Projects were the prime driver for business both before the purchase and with the new owner. The close relationship reflected the fact that for years both firms had been using similar project management procedures and shared similar views on how projects should be run. Just before the merger, the PMOs were spread out over different business units, but at the time of interviews, they had been moved to the same office area. Prior to this, The Armour depended almost entirely on a single client, whereas new clients are now located in many different countries. This has been a challenge for this high-tech firm which was dedicated almost entirely to servicing local needs when it needed to become a global competitor.

4.6.2 Transformation of the PMO

A few significant changes took place after the merger in 2005. The first change was the new owner's larger interest in the control of performance and a greater interest in the detailed reporting of progress. This was partly due to a difference of company culture and to a more competitive market situation. Under the new owner, the PMO had to consider influences of fluctuating currencies in their reporting, something they had never done in detail that was suddenly required due to a keener awareness of cost control.

In order to create a better view of the project management portfolio, bi-weekly review meetings were organized around a set of white boards, reporting progress, deviation, stage-gates and the green, red or yellow progress status of the different projects in the portfolio. The bi-weekly meetings were enhanced by two actions. The first was on a structural level, organizing the PMOs under the same business unit. The second one was sharing office space with the old PMO. This had a positive effect on the organizational learning and the possibility of sharing knowledge between projects.

With the reorganization of the PMOs into one business unit came other changes, one of which was a shift to a greater focus on the product life cycle within the operation. To enhance this, the unit was divided into four groups: Configuration, Quality, Projects and Services. The first worked with the systems integration of the products; the second focused on quality issues and documentation; the third dealt with the delivery and development of projects; and the fourth focused on the development of products for the market and on how to support them with services and maintenance programs. The new unit consisted of about 150 persons, of which 120 were project managers. See Table 4.11.

Table 4.11. The Armour: PMO Transformation

		PMO TRANSFORMATION #10
Conditions	External drivers	From single to multiple clients
		Change in the global market and how business was run
	Internal drivers	New owner who previously had one important client
	Issues	Knowledge sharing between PMOs
		Different internal control principles with new owner
PMO Before	Structural characteristics	PMOs different at different business units
	Most important functions	Methodology, standards and tools
The Transformation	Difficulty of implementation	Fairly easy, using similar project management procedures and relying on working relationship between old and new management
PMO After	Structural characteristics	One PMO for the firm
		Project office includes four units: Configuration, Quality, Projects and Services
		Greater emphasis on the product life cycle
		100% of project managers
	Most important functions	Monitor performance with great detail
		Methodology, standards and tools across business units
		Multi-project management
		Bi-weekly review meetings
Consequences	Impact in issues	Portfolio management implemented
		Easier for top management to view progress within the new PMO
	New issues	

4.7 Organization 7: "The Hospital"

4.7.1 Organizational Context

"The Hospital," as indicated by its name, was a hospital in a metropolitan area. The Hospital was recognized for its research and teaching, and was considered a new organization with an established history (the result of a merger of two hospitals, both with international reputation for their research and clinical performance, one being younger and the other older and well-established). The merger was driven by the owners with an aim to reduce costs and improve performance. The Hospital involved a large proportion of its staff in research, with natural tensions between clinical work and academic activities in the labs. The two sites were located within a 20-minute car drive from one another.

In one of the previous hospitals, there was an active commitment to project management as an important management principle. In this hospital, project management was implemented through a series of medical technology projects.

These projects often had an important IS/IT component. In this climate, a PMO was built up to support project managers with tools, procedures and later with project portfolio tools to keep track of ongoing projects. In the promotion of project management, the PMO worked to maintain ongoing networking meetings between project managers and advise about project management training. There was a network of about 80 project managers that participate jointly in different activities. The structure of project sponsorship for different projects was not clear and projects could be started at local clinics or by the administration and without the PMO's knowledge.

4.7.2 Transformation of the PMO

With the 2004 merger, the PMO was organizationally moved down and shifted into the IT department. This may appear as a natural move given that they worked intensively with IT-related projects. However, they also increasingly worked on more, different types of projects. At that time, the PMO had about eight to ten projects and it had a reputation outside the organization for having a network of project managers outside the PMO. People participated in their meetings to discuss issues related to stakeholders, mentoring, benefit analyses, risks, and project success index. PMO employees were also involved in the development of larger project management procedures with other hospitals and public organizations and later on with the development of a lighter version for medical clinics.

The PMO went from a fairly central point in the younger hospital to a more peripheral point after the merger which was accelerated when a new CEO came to the organization in 2007. The new CEO focused completely on process efficiency, reduction of costs, and division of labor for the 15,000 employees, and moved projects and their management to a very low priority. One strategic goal was to build a new hospital to replace the old hospital buildings. Along with the creation of the new hospital were many simultaneous smaller and larger projects necessary to successful construction. The new CEO wanted to create a program office for many of its larger undertakings. In doing so, the mandate of the PMO was transformed to support lesser responsibilities. See Table 4.12.

Table 4.12. The Hospital: PMO Transformation

		PMO TRANSFORMATION #11
Conditions	External drivers	Owners want to reduce costs
	Internal drivers	Merger between two organizations
	Issues	A PMO that had managed the project management procedures and organized a network of voluntary project managers
PMO Before	Structural characteristics	The PMO has a chair in the management team at one of the hospitals
	Most important functions	Methodology and network of project managers
The Transformation	Difficulty of implementation	A move from a strategic position down to the IT department
		A new CEO that dislikes projects and project management
PMO After	Structural characteristics	Transfer of the PMO to a different part of the organization
		Merger between organizations
	Most important functions	PMOs work to create recognition via network of project managers around the hospital
Consequences	Impact on issues	Project management culture was present in limited number of pockets
	New issues	CEO considers a program office
		Disappointment and worry about the future of the PMO

4.8 Organization 8: "The Data Warehouse"

4.8.1 Organizational Context

"The Data Warehouse" was a subsidiary of an international finance and insurance company. The parent firm operated around the globe and had done so for many decades. The Data Warehouse was part of a group of larger IT-solution providers that were bought over 20 years ago, after which data storage and IT infrastructure became increasingly important. The Data Warehouse was responsible for hardware and hardware solutions for the different financial products developed by the different market divisions. Compared to the overall organization, The Data Warehouse was a small organization within a large organization, even though it had an important function in making it possible to run applications and to store data generated by the different products. It was located next to one of the large regional offices.

The Data Warehouse had for many years acted partly as a service unit for the other business units. One problem had been that project managers worked for The Data Warehouse and used their own project management procedures. Projects were sometimes started without sponsors and without a steering committee. From time to time, it also happened that they had steering committees without projects. The organization of projects was sporadic and chaotic, making weak links between business benefits and projects. Operation was always a priority and projects were dealt with only when operations were running smoothly. At a neighboring operative unit, projects were run more strictly. Here a project management procedure was clearly established, a sponsor was always connected to a project before it started and there was an established project portfolio management system. In 2006, The Data Warehouse established a PMO and hired a new PMO manager with the aim of improving control over projects and establishing a standard for project management.

4.8.2 Transformation of the PMO

Around the time of the establishment of the PMO at The Data Warehouse a new owner entered the company. At first, the PMO was not very affected by the new owner and developments mostly concerned establishing routines. A project portfolio system was implemented, projects were given a sponsor before they started and regular meetings were organized to enhance the value of project management. In these meetings, progress and basic project management skills related to risk, benefit analyses and project performance were discussed.

After several months, the new owner began making new demands about how reporting should be done. It became clear that the new owner had management values based on the control of projects. The PMO and the organization itself were used to a fairly independent reporting tradition about deviations and progress and went to weekly meetings where they reported about risks. Over time, more reporting requirements for project cost and progress were put in place.

With these changes, new tools to improve collaboration and share documents were implemented. This was done to help the report structure in relation to available resources and to allow a better overview of the portfolio of projects. See Table 4.13.

Table 4.13. The Data Warehouse: PMO Transformation

		PMO TRANSFORMATION #12
Conditions	External drivers	New owner takes over the company
	Internal drivers	Project management structures and routines were immature
		New PMO manager
	Issues	Lack of link between projects and business benefits
PMO Before	Structural characteristics	Total lack of structure both on the project management level and on the portfolio level
	Most important functions	Network of project managers
The Transformation	Difficulty of implementation	New owner with new demands on reporting and structure
PMO After	Structural characteristics	Clear structures of projects by using a well-known project management procedure for projects and the portfolio.
	Most important functions	Work on creating a uniform way of working with projects
Consequences	Impact on issues	New control mechanisms create more stress to deliver new reports considered as fastidious
	New issues	Allowing PMO to become more strategic instead of being restrained by the problems of day-to-day operations

4.9 Organization 9: "The Store"

4.9.1 Organizational Context

"The Store" was a retail distributor that operates importing and warehousing operations and 400 retail outlets under the corporate banner. In addition, its products were sold through 400 retail agents. The Store employs 5,300 people and has an annual sales volume of 2.3 billion dollars. The vast majority of its 8,200 products were imported. Information systems were central to operations and many of the company's projects have a strong information technology (IT) component. The number of products and the level of sophistication of both the products and the clientele have increased significantly in recent years. This was associated with increased sophistication in marketing strategies and in information systems.

Prior to 1998, projects were executed in different business divisions and in the IT department with no centralized coordination. In 1999, the efforts to deal with the bug of changing millennium in systems, known as Y2K, required more coordination among units and the beginnings of a PMO were established. In 2000, under a new CEO, a decision was made to implement an enterprise resources planning (ERP) system relying primarily on a team of external consultants. The ERP implementation lasted for over three years and incurred significant cost overruns. A PMO was established to manage this enterprise-wide project. Projects other than the ERP implementation were carried out in the different departments under the direction of the unit managers. No formal project management was applied to these projects. The project managers had little accountability as the projects were being run under the direction of the unit managers. Projects rarely met objectives or delivery dates. The link between corporate strategy and the projects being executed was unclear. By the end of 2003, ERP implementation was coming to a close. This both freed up resources for many projects that had been waiting for the ERP system to be implemented and created a visible need to establish priorities.

4.9.2 Transformation of the PMO

A new CIO with a strong background in project management was appointed from outside the company in late 2003 and a new CEO was appointed in 2004. Both put a high priority on bringing the company's projects under control and in line with the business strategy. A new PMO was established and a PMO manager was recruited externally. The PMO, located in the IT department, was given responsibility for both IT and business projects. A project management methodology was put in place. The roles and responsibilities of both the functional and the project managers were clarified, not without considerable resistance from the functional managers.

Prior to 2004, the portfolio of the company's projects had not been managed as a coordinated whole. There were many projects and no clear vision of the whole portfolio. A strategic planning effort in 2004 identified 135 strategic initiatives and showed that the project portfolio needed to be better managed. A project governance structure with a steering committee for each project and periodic reporting to the company steering committee was established. Project portfolio management was implemented with a project classification and prioritization structure.

At the moment of interviews, prioritization and resource allocation were more in line with strategic objectives and the organization's capacity to deliver projects. Then, attention of the management turned to increasing the "velocity" of project delivery by controlling the scope of projects and by further reducing the number of projects underway at one time. The reduced number of projects provided more focus and put pressure on management for timely decision-making. Higher velocity also meant the deliveries were accelerated leading to faster realization of business benefits. Of the 30 to 40 projects in the pipeline only 20 were currently being executed. The others were either in preparation or were future projects that had not been authorized.

In 2007, a new PMO manager was appointed. He was again recruited from outside the organization in an industry with well-established project management traditions. With well-established portfolio management, the priority was to improve the performance of individual projects by increasing the rigor with which project management methods were applied. The nomination of the new manager and the change in focus were not considered as a transformation or a rupture, but rather as an evolution that was consistent with the direction set in 2004.

The effort to improve portfolio management continued with adjustments to make methods lighter and simpler. A new organizational role was emerging— that of portfolio manager. The PMO had the support of upper management, because it was seen to be delivering results. Through its involvement in portfolio management the PMO was seen as having a role in the company's strategic management. See Table 4.14.

Table 4.14. The Store: PMO Transformation

		PMO TRANSFORMATION #13
Conditions	External drivers	Increasingly sophisticated market
	Internal drivers	New CEO and CIO
	Issues	Poor project performance
		Lack of accountability
		Lack of link between projects and business benefits
PMO Before	Structural characteristics	PMO in name only
	Most important functions	Management of enterprise-wide project
The Transformation	Difficulty of implementation	Relatively easy; relied on support of upper management but encountered resistance from functional managers.
PMO After	Structural characteristics	Within IT department
		61% to 80% of projects
		100% of project managers
		Greater decision-making authority
		Greater accountability for project results
	Most important functions	Monitor project performance
		Methodology, standards and tools
		Multi-project management
Consequences	Impact on issues	Better project performance
		Portfolio management implemented with good results
		Greater credibility of PMO: participation in strategy implementation
	New issues	Functional managers need to redefine their role

4.10 Organization 10: "The Financial Group"

4.10.1 Organizational Context

"The Financial Group" was a group of companies in the financial services sector, primarily in banking and insurance services. The group was over 100 years old and had 40,000 employees and total assets of 144 billion dollars. This case study focuses on the program implemented in order to comply with the Basil II Accord. The program covered all the companies in the group, but the central organization was the banking services company. Regulations and interpretation of the regulations were emerging as the program unfolded. The program started in 2003. The case study focuses on the major restructuring in 2005. The program was scheduled to end in 2009.

The program started in 2003 and lasted for two years before a major restructuring took place. Two drivers contributed to the need to restructure, including poor performance and a major reorganization within the banking services company.

During the first two years, the program focused on a series of feasibility studies. A total of 50 million dollars was spent with no concrete deliverables. Each year the amount budgeted was not spent because no projects went to execution phases. The program was not considered important by business leaders throughout the organization. The program was run on annual budgets with no long-term plan, a project management culture was not in place, and there was no project management. The program seemed to be turning in circles. The perception was that two years had been lost while the final delivery date of 2009 had not changed.

4.10.2 Transformation of the PMO

In 2005, the governance structure at the level of the entire group of companies was reinforced. The banking services company restructured from a functional structure to a structure based on business units with significant power in the hands of the executives responsible for the business units. The program was successfully repositioned within this new structure. A senior executive at the level of the group of companies became the program sponsor. The new CEO of the group of companies positioned the Basil II Accord accreditation as a major corporate goal. The new executive sponsor was able to position the program as contributing to the business objectives of the executives responsible for the business units. Each of the companies in the group and each of the executives responsible for the business units in the banking services company were being held accountable for program benefits in their part of the organization.

While important changes were taking place at the level of corporate governance, changes were also being made at the program level. A new executive director was appointed to the program and the PMO in the fall of 2004. The program was benchmarked with other organizations undertaking this type of program. Following a consultant's audit, the program was reorganized into three sub-programs and a PMO with overall responsibility for the program and its integration. The PMO reported directly to the executive sponsor in the group-level governance structure. Each of the sub-programs had an executive sponsor and a steering committee. The people responsible for the business were directing the program and sub-programs and were responsible for business results.

The program had previously been organized to produce one deliverable at the end of the process. It was reorganized around many smaller deliverables and the ability to show business benefits throughout the program's life cycle. The project management methodology was reinforced. After the transformation, the program was perceived as doing appropriate projects and was supported by a project management culture.

The changes at the corporate and program level took over a year to implement. The changes at both levels were concurrent and interdependent. The result was a global transformation of all aspects of the program and its governance. See Table 4.15.

Table 4.15. The Financial Group: PMO Transformation

		PMO TRANSFORMATION #14
Conditions	External drivers	International regulatory requirements
	Internal drivers	Broad restructuring
		Change in the executive team and in the PMO's management
		Poor performance
	Issues	Lack of results
		Lack of organizational support for program
PMO Before	Structural characteristics	Weak structure with little program or project management
	Most important functions	Overall responsibility for program
The Transformation	Difficulty of implementation	A difficult starting point; Not an easy sell
		Easier after top-level support was obtained
		Difficult because many things had to be changed concurrently; required investment of time and strategy
PMO After	Structural characteristics	Reports to most senior level
		13-18 people in PMO
	Most important functions	Overall responsibility for program
		Internal customer Interface
		Strategic management
		Monitoring project and program performance
Consequences	Impact on issues	New legitimacy: support and accountability throughout the organization at all levels
		Clear vision
		Delivery proceeding as planned
	New issues	The structure was more bureaucratic

4.11   Organization 11: "The Telephone Company"

4.11.1   Organizational Context

"The Telephone Company" was a telecommunication service provider with annual revenues of 10 billion dollars. This case deals with the PMO in the business unit responsible for accounts with large organizations, which was a very competitive market. Projects were executed in a matrix organization with strong functional units. There were also important external suppliers. Team members were not allocated full-time to projects.

Traditionally, the company has been oriented towards sales, and often experienced difficulty delivering what had been sold. In recent years, there has been a change from delivering telecommunication hardware to delivering business solutions that are software-dependent. Solutions have also become more complex and more customized to the needs of individual clients.

A separate unit was responsible for large accounts in each of the two major geographic regions served by the company. There were important linguistic and cultural differences between the two regions. Each of the units in region A and B had a PMO, but both the methods being used and the overall level of development were quite different in each. Many large organizations operating in both regions have observed the differences in operational methods in each region. This came to be seen as a business issue that contributed to the need for a transformation.

At the time of interviews, the entire company had undergone significant changes in the composition of its senior management team. Improvements to business results had become an important focus. In line with these changes, a new president with experience in the software industry was appointed to the business unit responsible for accounts with large organizations. This president considered project management to be a competency that was important for his business and plans to improve project management maturity and standardization of methods across both regions.

PMOs have been in place in both regions since the late 1980s. Each regional PMO had its own methods. In 2000, the project management processes of the PMO in region A were ISO certified. This was at least in part a response to interest expressed by large customers in this regional market. Since 2000, the processes and methods have been continuously improved. Internal audits and annual external audits have been an important part of the continuous improvement effort. From interviews, it appeared that the people responsible are quite proud of this long-term commitment to continuous improvement. The methods and processes were not always uniformly applied but were considered advanced and well-adapted to the context.

The PMO in region B had not invested as heavily in project management methods and processes. Quality standards such as ISO were not as popular in this region and customers did not ask for them. As a result, they were not implemented.

An external consultant evaluated the maturity of project management in each region and concluded that region A was more mature than region B; region A was evaluated at level 3, while region B was at level 2.4 on a 5-point scale. Each PMO did, however, have its strong points; region A was seen as stronger on methodology, while region B was seen as stronger on leadership.

4.11.2 Transformation of the PMO

Under the new president, an important transformation took place in early 2007. The objective was to have a common vision in the management of projects and uniform procedures between the two regional PMOs. A new Enterprise PMO was created with the mandate to standardize the methods used across both regions. The Enterprise PMO was responsible for project management processes, support, and quality assurance. Each regional PMO was responsible for the implementation of a solution in the site of a customer. The new president considered the PMO not as a cost center but as a value creator.

Since early 2007, the focus has been on coming to agreement on which processes, methods and documents will be adopted for use in both regions. This has required considerable effort over a year and a half, with linguistic and cultural differences adding to the difficulty. Agreement has been reached on the processes and documents to be used, but much work remains to harmonize project management across both regions. Region A views this as a step backwards, as its members considered their methods to be more advanced than those that will now be implemented across both regions. In addition, the transition period created disturbances that disrupt processes that were working well.

Despite these considerations, the transformation was seen as necessary in order to produce better business benefits across both regions. One indication of the greater focus on business benefits was the change in monitoring project status. Previously, the focus had been on delivering the required scope on time, while little consideration was given to costs. Now profitability is the issue; costs are reported and followed closely by upper management. See Table 4.16.

Table 4.16. The Telephone Company: PMO Transformation

		PMO TRANSFORMATION #15
Conditions	External drivers	Increasingly sophisticated products
		Competitive market
	Internal drivers	New president
		New business orientation
	Issues	Poor project performance
		Lack of consistency between two regional offices
PMO Before	Structural characteristics	A very different PMO in each region
		101-500 projects, 80%+ of projects, 76%+ of PMs, some authority
	Most important functions	Region A very strong on methodology
		Region B methodology less strong
The Transformation	Difficulty of implementation	Support of new president eased transition; difficulty arose from finding consensus between two offices with different cultural and linguistic characteristics
PMO After	Structural characteristics	Same projects and PMs
		More authority
		More staff
		More accountability for results (project and business)
	Most important functions	Monitor project performance
		Methodology, standards and tools
Consequences	Impact on issues	Learning process to get the best from two regions
		Greater accountability for business results
		Impact difficult to evaluate because transformation still in progress
	New issues	Competition between the two regions to be recognized as the best

4.12 Organization 12: "The Power Company"

4.12.1 Organizational Context

The focus of this case study was on the Department of Energy Efficiency within a national utility company, "The Power Company." A new CEO has been in place since 2005. The mission was to reliably supply electricity to customers. At the heart of this mission was the equilibrium between supply and demand from a market that goes outside national boundaries and where there is an important variation dependent on seasonal temperature. Investments planning should recognize a diversity of means that will maintain equilibrium from the supply side with new barrages, wind energy, old barrage rehabilitation and from the demand side with energy efficiency programs. The latter programs take advantage of recognition of the global warmth and the need to use energy more efficiently.

The social focus for energy efficiency has manifested in waves since the 1960s. The last wave started in 2004 and was grounded in the dramatic situation of the global warming and the contribution of The Power Company in energy efficiency. Since then, the Department of Energy Efficiency faced challenges with constant growing targets in terms of economy of kilowatt/hour regulated by government. The very first programs of energy efficiency often harvested low-hanging fruits, and results were generally easy to collect. After that point, however, more efforts are required to reach results in terms of economy of kilowatt/hour. Indeed, during the transformation, programs were being selected with caution and projects were being managed more efficiently in order to gain the benefits for which they were launched.

4.12.2 Transformation of the PMO

This PMO transformation led to profound changes in the implementation of project management culture while keeping the same PMO director in place. The Department of Energy Efficiency was split into small business units, each one responsible for a client base. The first PMO was put in place in 2004 with new responsibilities for kilowatt/hour economy. The director was a proponent of PMOs and believed strongly in the project management philosophy to deliver results. The PMO was located at the same level as the small business units. At that time, almost nobody in the Department of Energy Efficiency was aware of what project management could be as a discipline. Employees were specialists working on operational activities who were then asked to work on projects. A project coordinator from a functional unit was assigned to a project. This person was chosen based upon the project content, not on project management knowledge or capabilities.

This PMO's main focus was to produce a project management framework to document the project management processes, deliverables and responsibilities. Many different tools and templates were also made available to complement the framework. The framework was developed from a strict best practices perspective without consulting any stakeholder. The PMO manager, as the proprietary of this framework, then imposed these prescriptions on people who were working on projects.

The mandate for implementing the first PMO was given to an outside consultant, which created difficulties within the organization. Employees felt the consultant did not take their contributions seriously and did not incorporate the ideas and concerns of the whole company into proposed changes. The strong negative reaction to this consultant led to his/her replacement by an internal manager.

The project management framework was used to control projects. This approach involved imposing a rigid method of managing projects over the Department of Energy Efficiency. In parallel, management of operational programs was left with no specific strategies and objectives to manage a wide range of different stakeholders. This dual management approach created confusion at the management team level and dissatisfaction regarding the perception of excessive control associated with the project management framework. Adding to the issue mentioned above, the PMO was considered too bureaucratic. One project manager said that when following the project management framework, a number of templates had to be completed though they weren't being understood: "Every person had to work first for the PMO without considering the business reality."

After two years of tensions and conflicts, the PMO had to change. In terms of business challenges, government continued to put pressures on the Department of Energy Efficiency in order to reach more aggressive targets. The working climate was negative and made it difficult for employees to work efficiently and effectively.

From an organizational structure perspective, the mandate of the PMO was split into three parts, which were then located at a lower hierarchical level as a functional unit but under the same manager. Meanwhile, the management team of the whole Department of Energy Efficiency has been almost completely renewed, with only two out of seven keeping their seats.

Within this new PMO, the major focus has been maintained on the project management framework. While its value has been acknowledged over the Department of Energy Efficiency, many changes had to occur in order for this new tool to begin contributing to department objectives. The most important move related to the ownership of the project management framework. The functional manager, under which the PMO was located, worked to encourage ownership among all managers, so they would be engaged to support their people. At the same time, the framework was made more flexible and its application, relaxed. For example, this framework was applied to all activities of the department, including the management of operational programs. From there on, there was a single approach for management of all activities within the department, projects or operational programs. The portfolio management has also evolved. In the previous situation, the portfolio was more or less an integrated collection of all projects. With this new PMO, portfolio management has provided a strategic view on optimized portfolio. Even communications from the PMO changed to produce value added information on the project portfolio for the governance board. These changes were made with the intention to bring the PMO to work at a more strategic level and to help the management team make better decisions regarding projects.

In this department, the project management culture was implemented quietly even though there were still no "true" project managers. The role of project coordinator was reinforced and moved on to the PMO. There was an intention to introduce, in the medium term, a "project manager" role within the PMO, as this role was being more accepted. The management team of the Department of Energy Efficiency has accepted that it takes time to make these changes happen, as mentioned by the PMO manager: "It doesn't happen naturally. It takes time. It is normal with these types of changes, that it takes time to succeed in implementation." See Table 4.17.

Table 4.17. The Power Company: PMO Transformation

		PMO TRANSFORMATION #16
Conditions	External drivers	Growth of social responsibility for energy economy
		Government fix targets and control achievement
	Internal drivers	Growth of number and value of projects
		Strategy of the company to integrate new challenges
		Business transformation: from operational to project
	Issues	PMO was seen as "police;" bureaucratic framework
		Implementation issues: conflicts
		Rigid way of developing project
		Lack of project management culture
PMO Before	Structural characteristics	Functional unit
	Most important functions	Methodology, standards and tools
The Transformation	Difficulty of implementation	Very difficult during first implementation
		Smooth for transformation
PMO After	Structural characteristics	Within a functional unit, at a lower level
		Larger % of projects
		More decision-making authority
		Larger funding
		Better organizational culture
		More accountability for project management results
	Most important functions	Monitor project performance
		Multi-project management
		Customers interface
		Strategic management
		Specialized tasks
Consequences	Impact on issues	Project management culture was increasing
		Work climate improvement
		Solidarity within the management team
	New issues	No "true" project managers

4.13 Organization 13: "The Engineering Company"

4.13.1 Organizational Context

"The Engineering Company" was a local office of an international private company that was fifty years old. It was a worldwide engineering company which specializes in three markets: mining and metal, energy and infrastructure. In each market, The Engineering Company offered services, including project management as an integrative way of delivering projects with success. At the time of interviews, the market for mineral exploration and metal production was in an unprecedented expansion due to the growing need for resources from Asian economies. The global capital project portfolio managed by the project delivery group was worth 50 billion dollars. The firm employed nearly 10 thousand employees in both hemispheres.

Since its beginning, this consulting company has developed continuously based on a global tendency for annual growth in demand for ore through 2002. More specifically, the company has developed new markets from the mid-90s in the south hemisphere. This strategy helped the company to overcome the downturn in the economy that affected most countries in the Northern Hemisphere. Since 2003, economic recovery and growth in the demand for ore from developing countries have contributed to constant growth as measured by number of employees.

As an engineering consultant company, projects were realized for external customers. Typically, there were two different *types* of PMOs within this company: regional project offices dedicated for a unique customer, often on the customer site or nearby and a unique PMO at the head office responsible for multiple customers with a focus on large projects. This transformation refers to the PMO at the head office, which was qualified as one of the regional hubs.

4.13.2 Transformation of the PMO

The first PMO was created in 2008 to address a need for the coordination of constant growth in the number and value of projects. There were four major challenges that led the PMO to a transformation. First was a lack of precision in roles and responsibilities in project management. There was a consensus among interviewees that the organizational chart was not clear. The question: "Who's my boss?" couldn't be answered easily. They answered, "it depends," and were not able to clearly state one name. All interviewees also emphasized that their position was flexible. They had one position, but they went where help was needed within the local center or even through the worldwide company. The hierarchy, they all said, was not important; the relationship with the customer was what counted.

The second challenge was the increase in project complexity. The complexity originated with geographical distribution of raw material and environmental issues. Getting access to raw material was more and more complex, as intact deposits were located in regions that were difficult to access. The logistics of extracting deposits became more complex, as did environmental regulations and issues that were not originally part of the company's process.

The third challenge concerned the quality and security of The Engineering Company's projects, which were oriented to environmental and audit issues and, particularly, on the security of machines. The company had recognized that employees represented their unique assets and from interviews, employees seemed to be proud of their company. The turnover was low, as most employees stayed within the company for their entire career. As the regional PMO director said: "It is part of the management philosophy to keep people and not to hire consultants or employees on a contractual basis."

The fourth challenge was the lack of qualified resources in project management. This reality was common to the overall industry due the continuous growth of the market. It was very difficult to train newcomers to the internal project management culture, processes and tools. When the number of employees was relatively low, the transfer to newcomers was easy and feasible. A regional manager within a business unit said: "Everybody knew the processes and they were sharing their knowledge with a small team. Now it is impossible. The number of experienced people is not large enough to train the newcomers."

After the PMO transformation, the PMO director had three major responsibilities: project quality and standardization, project performance and maintaining the career path of people working on projects. She argued: "I am responsible for making people happy in their job, and there are challenges." This transformation included the recognition of project management as a discipline along with other engineering–based disciplines.

This situation led to the formalization of a methodology and then to the creation of the PMO. Everybody within the company then shared the same methodology and processes through an intranet site. "It works! [...] and it makes unanimity. There is a general agreement about it." Interestingly, the methodology was then also used to train customers, and was presented in the public website of the company. But this wide use of a unique process for managing projects was not put in place to please the regional PMOs, where they are managing small projects for a unique customer. This was seen as bureaucratic approach from the Head Office. See Table 4.18.

Table 4.18. The Engineering Company: PMO Transformation

		PMO TRANSFORMATION #17
Conditions	External drivers	Economic growth from emergent economies
		Worldwide growth in demand for resources
		Environment and security of and for workers
	Internal drivers	Value for project management increased
		Customer centered
		Created a new entity for the coordination of project portfolio and nominated a new Director
		New president and CEO
		More geographical complexity in projects
	Issues	Developing long-term relationship with other customers
		Commitment to project management as a formal discipline
		PMO costs
		Fuzzy structure: some people are uncomfortable
		PM competencies lacking
PMO Before	Structural characteristics	Informal, under the executive
	Most important functions	Monitor project performance
		Multi-project management
The Transformation	Difficulty of implementation	Easy
PMO After	Structural characteristics	Central, under the executive
	Most important functions	Methodology, standards and tools
		Competencies in project management
Consequences	Impact on issues	Clarification of roles and responsibilities through PMO structure
		Complexity of project managed through defined project management processes
		Lack of competencies in project management: training in project management through a new tool
	New issues	Bureaucratization of the project management from the viewpoint of the local centers

In conclusion, the descriptions of these 17 PMO transformations tell different stories, each with its own particular characteristics. These stories constitute the raw material from which qualitative analyses were undertaken. Results from case study analyses are presented in the next chapter.

CHAPTER FIVE: RESULTS FROM CASE STUDIES

In the previous chapter, the 17 case studies were described and summarized. This chapter presents the results of the analysis of these case studies using the conceptual framework described in Chapter Two. The empirical study aims at obtaining data which will enable a process analysis. For this study, PMOs are experiencing a process of transformation as the agent of change. The authors adopted a constructivist approach, meaning that the phenomenon, here the PMO, is a complex object evolving in interaction within a context. In other words, the PMO and its context construct themselves over time through a transformation process.

When looking at the process side, the focus is no longer on the description of each individual PMO, but rather on the transformation from the original PMO to a new PMO. Therefore, the unit of analysis is the organizational transformation of a PMO. The sample is made up of 17 "organizational transformations" of existing PMOs.

Results from the analysis are presented in two parts. The first part concentrates on the drivers of a PMO transformation. A typology of drivers that led to the transformation is proposed. The second part presents three patterns of change observed in the case studies, which bear on the overall transformation process from the prevailing conditions to the resulting PMO and the consequences of the change.

5.1 Typology of Drivers

The conceptual framework for capturing the PMO transformation process is based on a continuous cycle of conditions, structures and outcomes of change which was presented in Section 2.4. The conditions, as drivers of change, were determined after extensive review to have varying degrees of importance. In each case study, significant drivers for a PMO change have been codified in a grounded theory approach, allowing the conditions to emerge from the actual interviewee comments. This method was presented in Section 3.1. An analysis of the 17 transformations revealed 35 drivers, which we clustered under six groups of drivers:

- External events
- Internal events
- Issues related to organizational context
- Issues related to project management process
- Issues related to human resources
- Issues related to performance

Figure 5.1 presents the typology of these six groups of drivers. The six groups and the thirty-five drivers and their definitions are listed in Appendix C.

Figure 5.1. A Typology of Drivers of PMO Transformations

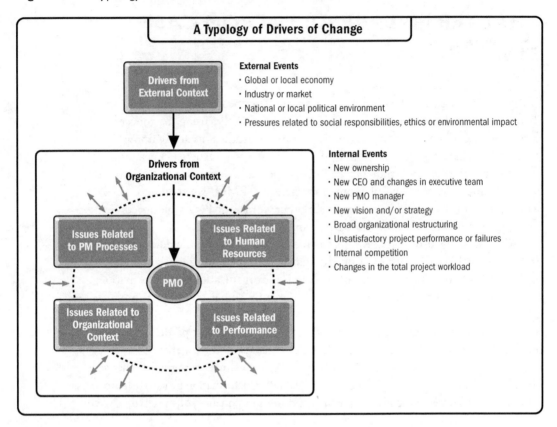

Table 5.1 presents the drivers that were present in the greatest number of cases. The number of cases in which the drivers were present is indicated in brackets. The results show evidence of the prevalence of internal drivers. Three factors may have led to an underestimation of the importance of external drivers. First, we have selected events from the external environment that had an impact on the PMO. The numbers reflect only a partial view of the global external environmental analysis. Second, we observed that interviewees in higher management positions often linked external events to a PMO transformation. For example, project managers generally focused on their project and were unaware of the global external environment. Third, an external event can have numerous impacts on the internal context of an organization over a long period of time. Despite these qualifying remarks, it is clear that most people interviewed attributed the changes in PMOs to events and issues that are internal to the organization.

Table 5.1. Most Frequent Drivers from Case Studies

EXTERNAL	INTERNAL				
1 **External Events**	**2** **Internal Events**	**3** **Organizational Context Issues**	**4** **Project Management Process Issues**	**5** **Human Relations Issues**	**6** **Performance Issues**
Industrial/ market (13)	New strategy (11)	Client and stakeholder relations (11)	Control of project portfolios (12)	Project management skills development (13)	Project performance (11)
	Reorganization (11)	Accountability for projects (10)	Standardized project management processes (11)		
	New CEO (11)				
	New PMO manager (10)				

In the first column of Table 5.1, the external context column shows that the industrial/market event was mentioned most often. In 13 cases out of 17, this driver played a role in the PMO transition. This led the authors to assume that reviewing only internal drivers is not sufficient to describe the organization holistically. External change in the industrial or market environment may have contributed to the PMO change decision. An example of this can be found in one of the case studies of a telecommunications organization after the dot-com bubble burst. The PMO was centralized with a strong control mandate over projects after the external driver affected its stability and effectiveness.

In the second column, there are four drivers under internal events. Projects are means to implement a business strategy (Morris & Jamieson, 2004); so structures such as PMOs become business structures (Pettigrew, 2003). Global reorganization, new CEO placements and new PMO manager hires are the three most important internal drivers. They often happen together. When such events occur, there is no reason to expect the PMO to remain stable, because the rest of the organization will be undergoing a global reorganization. This is an important result from our case studies that calls into question the stability paradigm for PMOs.

In the third column, issues within the organizational context show that relationships with clients and other stakeholders may lead to a PMO change. These issues refer to the organizational politics in which the PMO is embedded. A PMO from one of our case studies was almost completely forbidden from maintaining a relationship with the project clients. After a while, this PMO was disconnected from the client reality and lost its legitimacy in the face of business unit managers. The last driver in this column is the accountability for projects. PMOs might change to give more or less accountability to certain stakeholders. One example is given in a banking organization, when project managers were moved from the central PMO to business unit PMOs in order to give the business unit managers full accountability for project outcomes.

Considering the issues related to the project management process in the fourth column, one can conclude that control over the project portfolio is frequently mentioned as an issue leading to PMO change. The issues mentioned in our case studies refer specifically to the lack of legitimacy provided to a PMO so that it may influence the selection of projects to be included in the portfolio. Other drivers could be identified as potential issues, such as the allocation of resources between projects. The second issue in this group refers to the standardization of project management processes. This issue is often influential in one of two ways: not enough standardization or too much. In either case, it plays a role in PMO change. This point is taken into account in one of the PMO patterns of change described below.

In the fifth column, we can observe that the human side of the PMO is of great importance in the transition. Project manager skill development is a frequent driver in our case studies. The lack of these skills could lead to a change in the PMO. In our case studies, many interviewees highlight the major importance of interrelationship management skills, particularly when projects are done in a more international context. Finally, in the last column, the project performance issue was mentioned often as a driver for PMO change. Quite often, a PMO change is initiated after major project failures or problems. In some cases, a highly visible project failure was seen as an event. In others, project performance was an ongoing issue not related to any particular event. For this reason, project performance has been included as both an internal event and as an issue.

It should be noted that there are usually multiple interwoven forces at play at the same time. One driver may be more powerful, but alone, it may not lead to a PMO transformation. Less visible drivers may play an important role.

Several executive workshops utilizing this framework were in Canada, the USA, Australia and Europe. Feedback from participants confirmed not only the accuracy of the way the PMO transformation process was modeled but the relative importance of the drivers as well. Nevertheless, some executives expressed some reserve regarding the word "transformation." They argue for an "evolution" instead of a "transformation." The drivers may stay the same, but it is acknowledged within the organization that the PMO will evolve and it can often be managed that way. It is difficult to know whether the organizational realities being described are different or whether the organization or national culture may not accept that there are transformations in the same way that some cultures do not recognize the existence of conflicts. The 17 qualitative case studies were all recognized as transformations. However, there are certainly variations in the degree of change; they may vary from evolutionary to radical and disruptive. The survey questionnaire is designed to capture variations in the degree of change.

5.2 Patterns of Change

In this section we briefly present three patterns of change that were identified from the analysis of 17 case studies. These patterns **were not validated** in the sample from the quantitative phase of this research (see Chapter Seven). However, these results may be important to an understanding of the unique dynamics surrounding PMO transformation. See Chapter Nine for a complete discussion on these results.

The expression "patterns of PMO change" refers to the direction of movement from an initial to a new state. The PMO state can be described using its characteristics and functions. Comparing two PMO states allows the assessment of movement of a set of characteristics and functions expressed as "more of" or "less of." This definition of a change pattern could be useful in identifying a limited number of PMO transformations and relating them to changes in the external or internal environment or to specific issues. A pattern is defined basically as a model that is proposed for imitation; it can also fall under a complementary definition using the metaphor of the path of a plane or a football (Merriam-Webster, 2007). Using this definition, the PMO patterns are models of transformation paths.

The intention of this portion of the study is to identify high-level patterns showing the internal organizational logic that governs some PMO transformations. The results in the following paragraphs avoid detailed PMO characteristics and present each pattern individually. Often, these patterns occur simultaneously.

5.2.1 Pattern 1: Transition Based Upon the Level of Project Management Standardization

This pattern refers to project management standardization and is associated more specifically with the PMO function to *develop and implement standard methodologies, processes, and tools*. From our case studies, eight PMO transformations followed this pattern, which makes it the most prevalent. It could be described as a double transformation that evolves from an over-standardization of "one size fits all" project management to a flexible approach adapted to the project needs. The first transformation emerges from the acknowledgment of a lack in project management standardization; multiple ways of managing projects often coexist within the organization. Usually, projects are under the responsibility of multiple business or functional units. Each of these units has its own processes, methodologies, and tools. The impetus for project management standardization comes from two sources: the cost of duplication among units and the requirement that global portfolio management addresses common methods of managing projects, including the phases of the project life cycle or the definition of different types of costs in projects.

The resulting PMO mandate is to implement such project management processes, methodologies and tools throughout all the units of the organization. From these case studies, the strategy for implementing this standardization approach was often done without any change in management. Yet these PMOs gain the support of upper management to make standards compulsory for every single project. These cases reflected a real desire to follow project management standards after they were put in place, but dissatisfaction grew when experiencing the application of these standards within real projects. Not all projects fit within this rather rigid approach. More than that, the PMO was perceived as a bureaucratic entity, with project managers completing forms instead of leading their projects. In one of our cases, project managers were encouraged to be delinquent. Over time, tension and sometimes conflict emerge from this situation, which leads to a PMO transformation including a change in the standardization approach. The intensity of the issue, tension or conflict and the period of time between the changes in orientation vary from one organization to another.

The modified role of the PMO aims at implementing flexible standards depending on the type, complexity or risk of projects. This is often made possible with a more granular categorization of projects within the organization. Processes, methodologies, and tools are revised in order to be simpler and adapted to different realities. Some PMOs from our case studies make this standard renewal very participative. They invite stakeholders to participate in the elaboration of the new standards. This involvement makes change management easier and the adoption of standards desirable.

In this pattern we focus on PMO transformation regarding project management standardization. This type of change may be part of a more global change, and the management philosophy could also change. For example, transitioning from a compulsory application of standards to the offering of standards involves a profound change in the relationship between the PMO and their customers, changing the PMO's role from controller to advisor.

5.2.2 Pattern 2: PMO Playing Between Growth and Contraction

The organizations participating in this research were almost all in a growth situation. This might be interpreted within the context of the global economic situation of growth at the time of the investigation for countries participating in this research. The purpose of this pattern is to illustrate PMO transformation in a context of economic change in an industry or a company. The first case happens in telecommunications, where the IT bubble-burst in 2001 brought almost all companies in this industry into a difficult period, some of which were facing bankruptcy and other actions that limited their survival. The second company is a manufacturer, facing major changes in their product to serve new markets in China and India. Two major projects failed to deliver outcomes. In both of these organizations, the initial situation was the existence of multiple PMOs, basically one in each business unit. Each one was autonomous in their project management standards. When this situation was acknowledged at the executive level, both organizations engaged in project management centralization to create a single PMO. Both central PMOs were then involved in cost control management to a much greater extent than before. In the first example, the transformation was due to an external event, while an internal event gave the impetus for a PMO change in the second example.

This pattern makes sense by itself and is common for the whole organization. The duplication of efforts is not scrutinized within an organization experiencing strong growth, and money is of lesser concern. Duplication might also be encouraged in order to stimulate innovation, as in overlapping organization (Nonaka, 1990). But when it comes to survival, cost control becomes a priority. This result is aligned with Pettigrew (2003) where structuring occurs simultaneously with strategizing. In this sense, the present economic downturn could have impacts on business strategy and the number of projects undertaken by organizations (and consequently, on project management structures such as PMOs).

5.2.3 Pattern 3: PMO Going Agile

The third pattern for PMO change relates to global market competition. It addresses two specific features of project management: the flexibility of project management processes and methodology and time to market. Here we can observe from our case studies that firms are threatened by their competitors to reduce lead time in the delivery of new features. Project management processes can be implemented to support a sequential or waterfall approach, which could lead organizations to deliver outcomes only after the whole project is completely finished. Pressures from competitors push for shorter delivery. In these studies, a tendency for more experienced PMOs to adopt new methods borrowed from Agile methodology as described in Williams (2005) was observed. Under this approach, projects are split into several marketable pieces. These pieces are tested independently and can be offered on the market in order to bring quick benefits. In one specific case study, the PMO manager was asked to reduce the lead time from more than 12 months to less than two months. To do that, the PMO had to change most of its project management processes. It had to abandon the traditional stage-gate process with which the PMO was comfortable. An Agile approach was then implemented, with a process view of short-term deliveries with clear customer benefits. Even the role of the project managers changed. Instead of managing a single major project, the project managers were transformed into program managers leading multiple mini-projects. This fragmentation of projects into multiple pieces also called for solid integration management before and after the development of the project. It becomes essential that the new small projects can be managed and evaluated under the global product architecture. After all, the test of each piece doesn't guarantee the quality of the whole. Integration of all pieces into a unique product requires specific testing before delivery of a whole product.

5.3 Key Findings

Qualitative analysis on the 17 PMO transformations included in this research confirmed results that have already been anticipated from previous research on PMOs (Aubry, 2007). Key findings from case studies are classified under six themes.

1. *Identification of PMO transformation.* The analysis of the qualitative case studies confirms that the conceptual framework developed in Chapter Two helps understand the phenomenon on empirical ground. This process has emerged from previous research based upon a grounded theory approach,

where conditions-actions-outcomes form a cycle that repeats itself over time. In this research, the focus has been put on one transformation, but the process should be understood as a continuous dynamic. It calls for a systemic circular thinking where consequences become the conditions for the next cycle.

2. ***Systemic approach.*** Multiple, simultaneous external and/or internal events participate in the change, as do internal issues. There is no transformation triggered by a unique driver. It confirms that the PMO is part of multiple systems (business, social, political, technological, etc.) as suggested by Mintzberg (1989). With the increase in the number of projects within matrix-type organizations, the PMO could be seen as a central node connected to almost all domains within the organization. Political tensions seem to prevail at the interface with the rest of the organization, more specifically with the hierarchical structure. Hierarchy persists and causes innovative forms of organizing (Pettigrew, 2003). This result is in line with Larson (2004), who has scrutinized the interface between projects and the rest of the organization.

3. ***Notion of fit.*** Reconfiguration of a PMO is not random. Just the contrary, it seems as if the resulting PMO becomes more aligned with the organizational context. A particular set of characteristics comes together to form the new PMO configuration. One indicator for this alignment can be seen in the relative stability of the configuration until it reaches a point at which a certain level of misalignment will lead to change. This is in line with the results from Thomas and Mullaly (2008). From this research, it is not clear precisely how this alignment occurs, but future research might look at the configuration theory (Mintzberg, 1989) and the complementarities theory (Fenton & Pettigrew, 2000).

4. ***Typology of drivers.*** With the variety presented by the 17 case studies, it was possible to typify various drivers of change and conclude that it is more likely that PMO transformation be triggered by internal events or issues.

5. ***Limited number of patterns.*** Three patterns have been identified within the 17 case studies. More had been expected, particularly when considering a PMO life cycle. This result contradicts the linear orientation towards a better situation which is most often accepted as a description of PMO life cycle. The professional literature on PMOs suggests this type of progression towards progress (Kendall & Rollins, 2003). These three patterns were not validated in the sample within the quantitative phase of this research. Please refer to Chapter Seven for statistical analysis and to Chapter Nine for discussion on this result.

CHAPTER SIX: SURVEY RESULTS: DESCRIPTIVE STATISTICS

At this point, the conceptual framework (Chapter Two) and empirical results from 17 case studies (Chapter Five) confirm the pertinence of the PMO transformation process to answer the research question. The objective of the survey was to gain a better generalization of these results. The next three chapters present statistical analyses from the survey which was undertaken to validate results obtained from case studies (see Chapter three for more details on the methodology). This chapter presents results from descriptive statistics.

This chapter is organized in six sections as follows[1]. The first section presents general information on the survey and on demographics, giving a portrait of the respondents and their organization. The second section describes the change itself and the particular challenges from its implementation. The third section considers resulting PMO changes and the motives for such changes. After characterizing PMO change, this section presents the importance of external events, internal events and issues regarding PMO change. The fourth section focuses on what has been changed by examining the roles or functions of a PMO. The last two sections describe the structural characteristics of the PMO after the change and the key findings of the descriptive statistics.

6.1 General Information and Demographics

The survey was available from September 2008 through March 2009 in both English and French. The number of valid responses to the survey was 184. Of these, 22% were in French and 78% were in English. Appendix E summarizes sample demographics. Responses on PMO demographics (internal characteristics of organizations, including size, maturity level in project management, and others) showed similarity with earlier studies, (Hobbs & Aubry, 2007). This stability contrasts with the dynamics of PMOs.

6.2 Description of the Change and Its Implementation

This section presents the description of the change in terms of time and amplitude. Results from the implementation of the change are also presented.

---

1 A summary report has been produced to present descriptive statistics from the web survey. It is accessible at: www.pmchair.uqam.ca.

6.2.1 How Long Ago Was the Change Initiated?

Changes in the population have happened fairly recently, meaning within the last two years (69%). This is in line with the objective of this survey, as shown in Figure 6.1. The invitation to complete the survey asks about recent PMO changes. This is consistent with results from a 2005 survey, where 54% of the PMOs had changes initiated within the last two years.

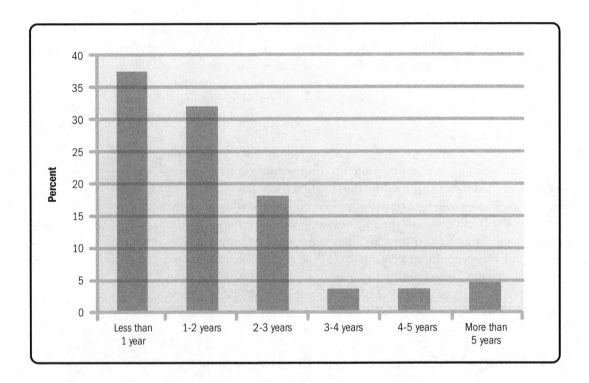

Figure 6.1. Time Passed Since PMO Change

6.2.2 The Amplitude of the Change

As shown in Figure 6.2, the amplitude of change follows a normal distribution but with a higher number indicating radical change (10%). It is worth mentioning that 71% of respondents evaluate an amplitude of 5 and more, the mean being 5.58 on a scale from 1 (minor change) to 9 (radical change). In this population, PMO changes are important and a large proportion of them would be considered major changes.

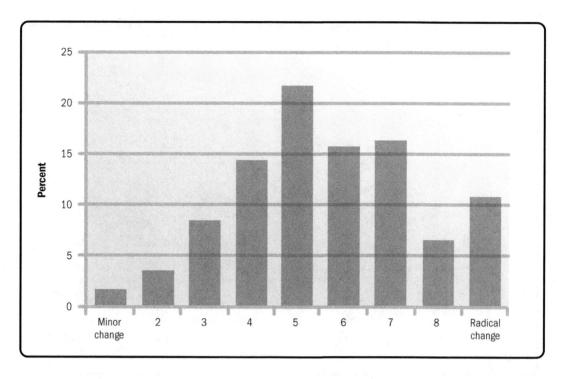

Figure 6.2. Amplitude of the Change

6.2.3 Implementation

PMO change implementations are reported to be quite difficult with 60% of implementations being at a level of difficulty of 6 or higher as shown in Figure 6.3 (mean: 5.82). When asked about change management, 52% of respondents answered that the PMO changes had change management processes, while 38% of respondents reported having no change management processes. It is interesting to note that PMO implementation is considered an organizational change that merits consideration of change management by more than half of the PMOs within this population. But there is still another 50% where implementation of a PMO change is not managed.

Implementation of PMO change varies quite a lot, but it is rarely instantaneous (3%). As shown in Figure 6.4, 22% of them take more than a year.

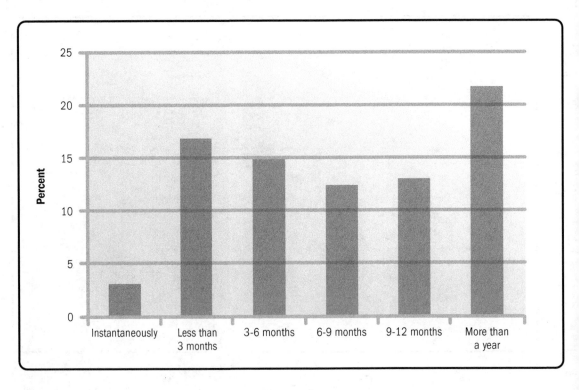

Figure 6.3. Difficulty of the Implementation

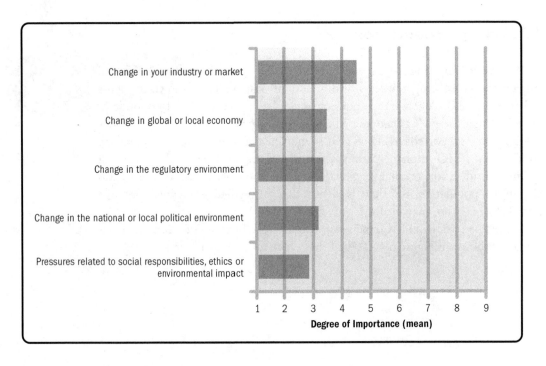

Figure 6.4. Time for PMO Change Implementation

6.3 Importance of Drivers of Change in PMO

The following section of the survey examined recent changes to PMOs. It focuses on reasons for these changes and their impacts, and only presents descriptive results. More complete statistical analysis is presented in Chapters Seven and Eight.

The importance of drivers leading to a PMO change is presented in three sub-sections, each one corresponding to the groups of drivers (see Section 5.1): *external events, internal events* and *issues*. Each figure presents the individual drivers in a descending order of importance, using the scale from the survey (1: no importance; 9: high importance). For ease of interpretation, the degree of importance is presented in four levels:

- Strong importance: from 7 to 9
- Great importance: 5 and 6
- Some importance: 3 and 4
- No importance: 1 to 2

6.3.1 The Importance of External Events as Drivers of PMO Change

This question aims at identifying the importance of external events as drivers of change in the PMO. Five events are proposed to capture the role of external environment. Figure 6.5 shows the mean of the important of each external event. Globally, external events do not seem to play a major role as drivers of PMO change even if they are present in the PMO's transformation landscape. The most important one is "Change in the industry or market" and has only some importance.

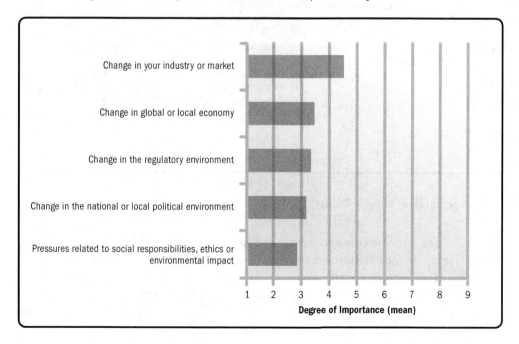

Figure 6.5. Importance of External Events

6.3.2 The Importance of Internal Events as Drivers of PMO Change

This question aims at identifying the importance of internal events as drivers of PMO change using a set of nine individual drivers. The graph in Figure 6.6 shows the mean importance for each internal event.

Four internal events have great importance. The most important one is a new vision or new strategy. It confirms the tight link between strategy and project management. As results show here, it also seems to play a role in PMO change. The second most important event refers to a broad organizational change within the organization. It confirms that the PMO is not an isolated island (Engwall, 2003). As organizations go through such restructuration quite often, there is no reason why the PMO will not be part of it. The third most important event shows the importance of project performance as a driver for changing PMOs. The fourth event, changes in total workload, might indicate that the PMO would benefit from adapting its capacity, by either an increase or a decrease, to the changing organizational need.

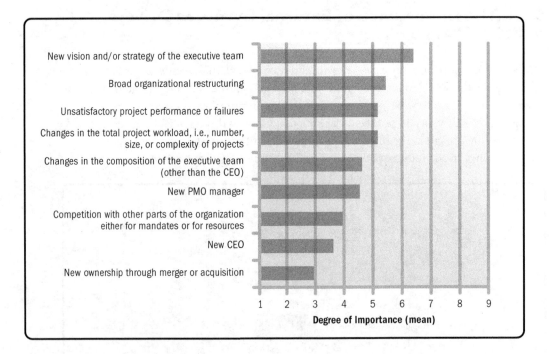

Figure 6.6. Importance of Internal Events

Five other events may have some importance in the PMO transformation. Change in the composition of the executive team and the arrival of a new PMO manager have almost the same level of importance. They both refer to a change in the management team and likely to a new philosophy of management. Competition with other parts of the organization, either for mandate or resources, can play a certain role in the PMO change. An example of this was found in an international company with multiple centers in different parts of the world. Centers in developing countries may offer products and services at lower costs, challenging their internal competitors for mandates. This event can lead to a change that improves the PMO's efficiency. The arrival of a new CEO is of some importance, but to a lesser degree than a new PMO manager or other executive. This could be interpreted to mean that the CEO is traditionally distant from the PMO in terms of strategy and business. The least important event is a change in the ownership of the organization. This may be because this event is less frequent.

Overall, the events vary in their average importance and they are seen as having, generally, little importance (with only one event that is over six). Typically, a combination of events leads to the change in a PMO. The factor analysis presented in Chapter Seven identifies patterns of events.

6.3.3 The Importance of Issues as Drivers of PMO Change

In the following section, results from the survey on the importance of issues are presented in four groups. In addition to external or internal events, other issues which contribute to the dynamics of PMO change. The importance of issues before the change, and the impact the PMO change has on these specific issues, follows the same pattern of distribution. In order to keep this summary to a reasonable size, only results from issues are reported here. The next four figures show the importance of issues using their mean importance. Figure 6.7 shows the importance of issues related to the organizational context.

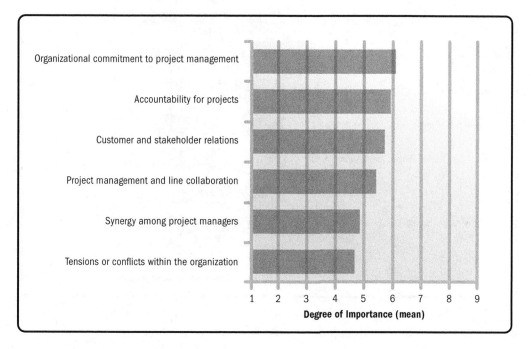

Figure 6.7. Importance of Issues Related to Organizational Context

Respondents assessed the importance of six issues regarding the PMO change. Four issues related to the organizational context were shown to be of great importance. The two most important are organizational commitment to project management and accountability for projects. Both of these issues refer to adhesion to project management within the organization. The issues of customer and stakeholder relations sometimes become an element of contention, as the management of customer or stakeholder interfaces can be a source of influence and prestige. The project management and line collaboration issues refer to tensions that are found in matrix structures or, more largely, at the interfaces between projects and the regular operations within an organization. PMO change can be undertaken to ease the tensions between project and line management.

Two other issues are of some importance regarding the PMO change. Respondents showed that the issue of synergy among project managers plays a role. This issue can be seen in relation to the decision to include or not to include project managers within the PMO. Previous research has shown that some PMOs do not include project managers, while some others do (Hobbs & Aubry, 2010). When they are not included, other mechanisms are recommended to encourage the synergy among project managers. The second issue of some importance refers to the tensions or conflicts within the organization. PMOs are part of the internal political system and as such are part of internal struggles for power. This agrees with observations from the qualitative data of the 17 case studies, where tensions and conflicts were part of almost all PMO changes.

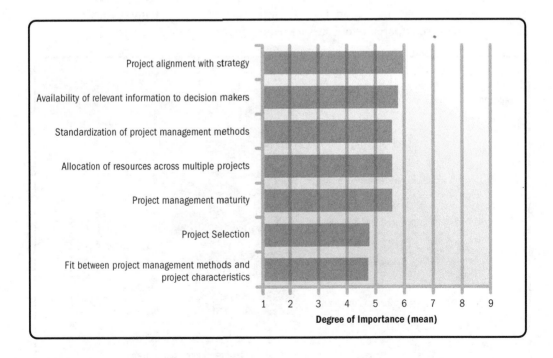

Figure 6.8. Importance of Issues Related to Project Management Processes

The importance of issues related to project management processes is presented in Figure 6.8. Five of the seven issues in this group are of great importance to the PMO change. The issue of project alignment with strategy indicates that a lack of alignment between strategy and projects may lead to a PMO change. The availability of relevant information for decision-making refers to the role a PMO can play by providing relevant and reliable information about projects. Standardization of project management methods can play a role in PMO change, which is often driven by either a lack of such standardization or an overabundance of standardization. Allocation of resources across multiple projects is an issue linked with resolving the equation between limited resources and a large number of projects or opportunities. The last issue within this group project management maturity. Change to the PMO may be related to the expectation that the PMO increase project maturity.

Two other issues are of some importance. The issue of project selection refers to project portfolio management, which can lead to a PMO change in order to reach more or less involvement in the selection of the right projects. The issue of fit between project management methods and project characteristics refers to the ability to adapt methods to the degree of complexity, risks, and other factors specific to the project. A lack of such granularity may lead to a PMO change.

Figure 6.9 presents the means of the three issues related to performance. Both project performance and business performance are important issues regarding the PMO change. The cost of the PMO is the least important issue of this group.

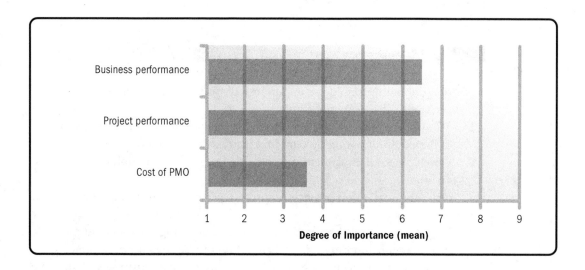

Figure 6.9. Importance of Issues Related to Performance

As shown in Figure 6.10, the issue related to project management skill level is the most important of the three issues related to human relations. Other issues, such as work climate and work-family equilibrium seem to play a less important role as drivers of PMO change.

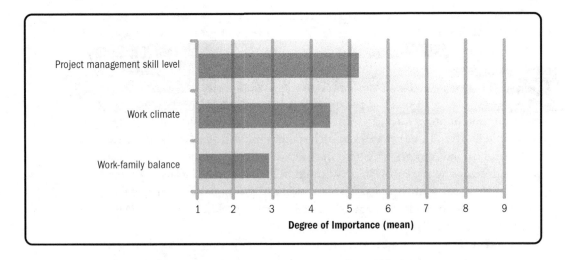

Figure 6.10. Issues Related to Human Resources

6.4 Changes to PMO Roles or Functions

In the third part of the survey, questions were designed to capture changes to the roles or functions this PMO fulfills. Results show that the importance of all functions typically improves after the change. This result may not be as positive as it appears at first glance; it may illustrate a positive bias from respondents to over-assess results from the PMO change.

6.4.1 The Functions a PMO Fulfills

The questionnaire assessed the importance of nine functions before and after the PMO change. These functions were:

1. Monitoring and controlling project performance, including the development of Project Information Systems and the reporting function
2. Developing and implementing standards, including methodologies, processes, and tools
3. Developing the competency of project personnel, including training and mentoring
4. Implementing multi-project management, including program and portfolio management, coordination, and allocation of resources between projects
5. Conducting strategic management, including participation in strategic planning and benefits management
6. Tracking organizational learning, including the management of lessons learned, audits, and monitoring of PMO performance
7. Managing customer interfaces
8. Recruiting, selecting, evaluating, and determining salaries for project managers
9. Executing specialized tasks for project managers, e.g., preparation of schedules

Figure 6.11 illustrates the importance of each function using the mean of the importance at two different moments: before the change and after the change. The two curves show a positive gap for each function. Overall, results show that the importance of all functions is greater after the change than it was before. This might be interpreted as a positive attitude toward the PMO changes from respondents.

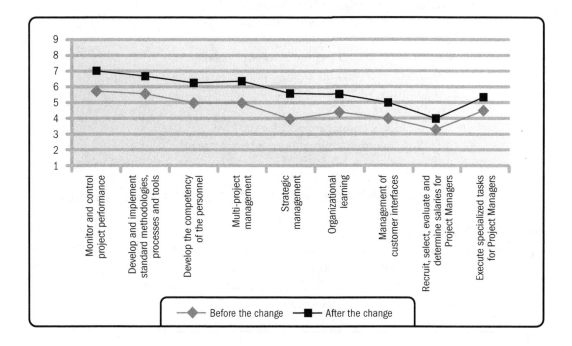

Figure 6.11. Change in the Roles or Functions of PMOs

6.4.2 Change in Supportiveness or Control of the PMO

A PMO fulfilling any of the functions listed in Figure 6.11 can be more or less supportive and can play its role with a more or less controlling approach.

Table 6.1 shows that both supportiveness and control have more importance after a PMO change.

Table 6.1. Change in Supportiveness and Control

	Before (mean)	After (mean)
Supportive	5.1	6.6
Controlling	4.6	5.9

6.5 Changes to PMO Structural Characteristics

The survey captures changes in the PMO using the following set of 10 structural characteristics:
- The PMO's location within the organization
- Interdependence with other PMOs
- The hierarchical level to which the PMO reports
- The PMO's access to top management
- Percentage of projects within the PMO's mandate
- Percentage of project managers reporting to the PMO manager
- Level of the PMO's decision-making authority
- Funding for the PMO
- Organizational culture support for the PMO
- The PMO's accountability for project performance

6.5.1 The PMO's Location Within the Organization

The PMO's location within the organization stays almost the same for operations, other functional units, human resources and finance. In Figure 6.12, we can see that the percentage of PMOs within IT diminishes after the change, while it increases for PMOs within business units, outside these units, and for those that report directly to a senior executive.

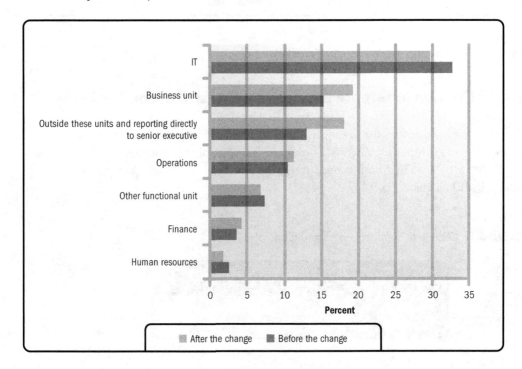

Figure 6.12. PMO's Location Within the Organization

6.5.2 Interdependence With Other PMOs

Respondents reported interdependence of the PMO they were describing with other PMOs. As shown in Figure 6.13, the percentage of PMOs having interdependencies increased after the change.

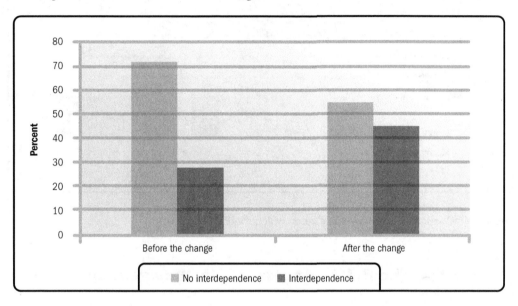

Figure 6.13. Interdependence with Other PMOs

6.5.3 Hierarchical Level to Which the PMO Reports

Figure 6.14 presents the results of the question of change on the hierarchical level to which the PMO reports. For almost half of the PMO transition (48%) there was no change. Only 11% indicated a change to a lower level, while 42% indicated a change to a higher level.

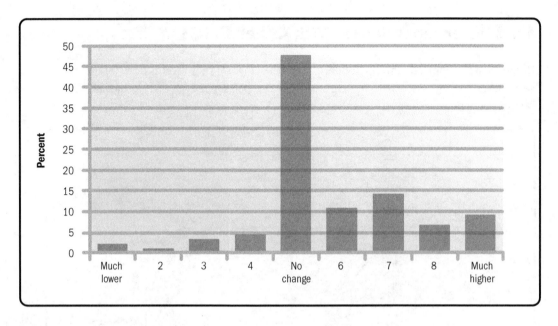

Figure 6.14. Change in Hierarchical Level to which the PMO Reports

6.5.4 The PMO's Access to Top Management

Changes often have an impact on the PMO's access to top management, but the pattern is not simple. In Figure 6.15, we see a regular curve from very difficult to very easy before the change. The curve for after the change shows a U-shape distribution with a first peak on the difficult side of the scale for 25% of the population, and a second peak on the opposite side for 16% of the population. After the change, 64% of respondents found access difficult compared to 51% before the change.

6.5.5 Percentage of Projects and Project Managers

The percentage of projects within the PMO's mandate increases significantly after the change, going from 59% to 72%. Similarly, the percentage of project managers reporting to the PMO manager increases from 37% before the PMO's change to 51% after the change. See Figure 6.16.

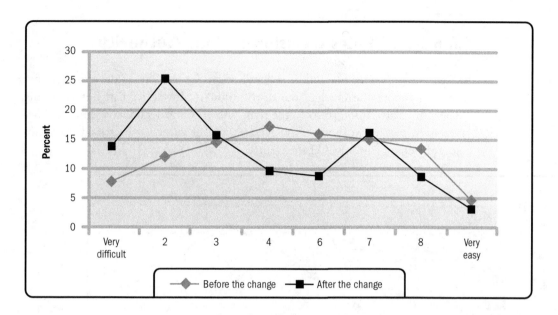

Figure 6.15. PMO Access to Top Management

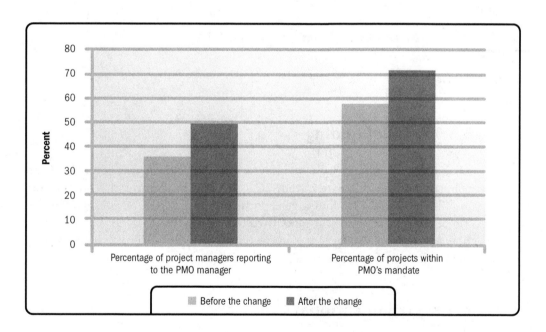

Figure 6.16. Percentage of Projects and Percentage of Project Managers within the PMO

6.5.6 The PMO's Decision-Making Authority

In Figure 6.17, we see two different distributions for the PMO's decision-making authority. Before the change, the distribution is almost regular, but after the change, the distribution shifts to the right, showing a general increase in the level of decision-making authority. The average level of authority increased from 4.5 before the change to 5.8 after the change.

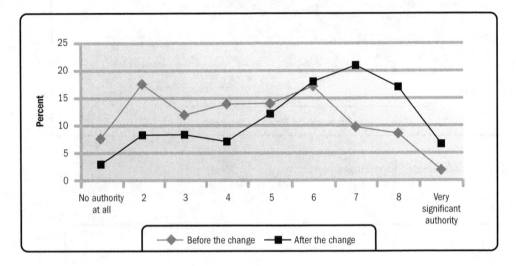

Figure 6.17. PMO's Decision-Making Authority

6.5.7 PMO Funding

As shown in Figure 6.18, the funding of the PMO is adequate for 42% of the population before the change, while 24% of respondents answer that funding was insufficient, while 18% find it generous to various degrees. Surprisingly, almost 2% of respondents find that funding of the PMO is overly generous. The curve after the change is similar to the one before the change. The PMO change doesn't seem to have an impact on the PMO's funding.

6.5.8 Organizational Culture

Figure 6.19 shows the extent to which the organizational culture supports the PMO. Typically, this increased after the change, which indicates that respondents perceived the change as positive. The mean value increased from 4.3 to 5.9 after the change.

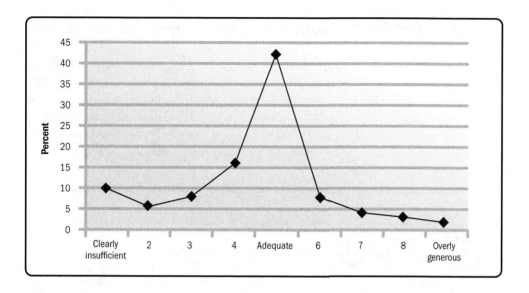

Figure 6.18. Funding of the PMO

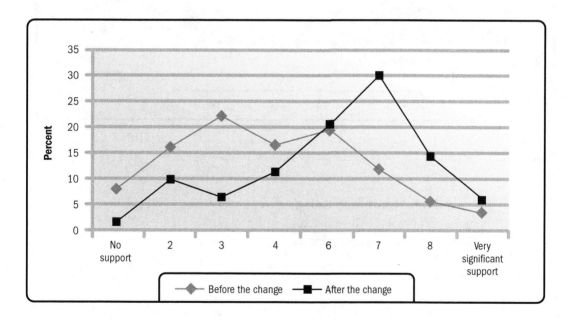

Figure 6.19. Support of Organizational Culture

6.5.9 PMO's Accountability for Project Performance

The survey included two questions covering aspects of accountability for project performance: project management (scope, cost & schedule) and business (benefits). The distributions for accountability for project management performance are quite different before and after the change; before, few PMOs had significant accountability, while after the change, most PMOs had such accountability. See Figure 6.20. The mean increased from 4.3 before the PMO change to 6.0 after the change.

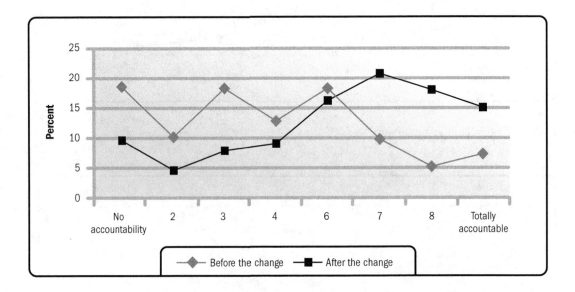

Figure 6.20. Accountability for Project Management Performance

Distributions before and after the PMO change also show a shift toward more accountability for business performance. See Figure 6.21. Means show an increase in the business accountability from 3.0 to 4.6.

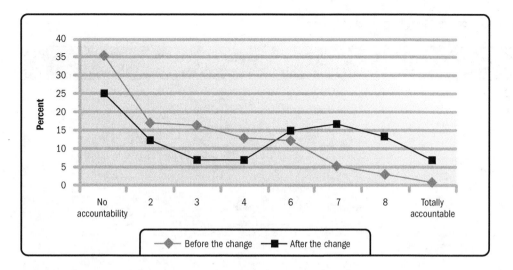

Figure 6.21. Accountability for Business Performance

6.6 Key Findings

Some insights on PMOs in transition can be concluded from the descriptive statistics previously presented.

1. Responses regarding PMO demographics (internal characteristics of organizations such as their size, the maturity level in project management, and others) showed similarity with earlier studies, including Hobbs and Aubry (2010). The stability of these aspects contrasts with the dynamics of PMOs.

2. Changes in PMOs are significant, and their implementation is apparently quite difficult.

3. Although a PMO transformation is a significant organizational change, only approximately 50% are implemented using an organizational change management process.

4. Multiple events and issues play a role in the PMO transition. No single driver is at a very high level of importance. This reinforces the assumption of the interweaving of multiple reasons that lead to a PMO change. Table 6.2 provides the list of the most important drivers, ones that may have the potential to lead to a PMO change.

5. By examining PMO functions and characteristics that describe what has changed, it is possible to observe that the level of their importance after the PMO change is reported to be greater. As stated earlier, there may be a positive bias toward these questions; respondents may have an overall tendency to over-assess benefits from the PMO change. The single characteristic showing a negative change is access to upper management, which seems to be more difficult after a PMO change.

Table 6.2. List of the Most Important Drivers

Groups of Drivers	Events and Issues Having Great Importance
Internal events	New vision and/or strategy of the executive team
	Broad organizational restructuring
	Unsatisfactory project performance or failures
	Changes in the total project workload
Issues related to organizational context	Organizational commitment to project management
	Accountability for projects
	Customer and stakeholder relations
	Project management and line collaboration
Issues related to project management processes	Project alignment with strategy
	Availability of relevant information to decision makers
	Standardization of project management methods
	Allocation of resources across multiple projects
	Project management maturity
Issues related to performance	Business performance
	Project performance
Issues related to human resources	Project management skill level

CHAPTER SEVEN: SURVEY RESULTS: FACTOR AND CORRELATION ANALYSES

Continuing the analysis of the statistics from the web-based survey, the objective of the factor analysis and the correlation analysis was first to reduce the data based on the underlying structure and to identify patterns in the transformation process. The results of four factor analyses, performed on contextual events and issues leading to the PMO change, the nature of the change to the PMO and impacts after the change are presented. The presentation of the results of the factor analysis is followed by a correlation analysis of relations among the factors and between the factors and other contextual variables. The chapter ends with a summary of key findings.

7.1 Contextual Events Leading to a PMO Change

Conditions leading to a PMO change come from internal and external events and issues. Individual factor analyses were done for events and for issues. The factor analysis of events identified four factors, from which two can be considered reliable (these will be looked at in more detail; see Table 7.1). The first factor contains all five of the external contextual factors and has been given the label *external factors*. The interpretation of this factor is quite straightforward and refers to changes in the external environment of the organization. It is interesting that all these changes are statistically significant. They all represent pressure on the organization to adapt to demanding situations.

The second factor has been labeled *change in top management*. It is noteworthy that neither the appointment of a new PMO manager nor changes to the vision and/or strategy of the executive team are associated with this factor. Because of low values for the Cronbach alphas, the variables in the last two factors are regarded as orphan variables.

Table 7.1. Factor Analysis of External and Internal Conditions Driving Changes to PMOs

Survey Items	EVENT 1 External Events	EVENT 2 Change in Top Management	EVENT 3 NA	EVENT 4 NA
Change in global or local economy	**0.827**	0.005	-0.063	0.180
Change in your industry or market	**0.734**	0.037	0.011	0.281
Change in the national or local political environment	**0.607**	0.331	0.185	-0.088
Change in the regulatory environment	**0.646**	0.194	0.406	-0.110
Pressures related to social responsibilities, ethics or environmental impact	**0.689**	0.094	0.258	-0.040
New ownership through merger or acquisition	0.325	**0.528**	0.077	0.152
New CEO	0.069	**0.866**	0.075	-0.102
Changes in the composition of the executive team other than the CEO	0.021	**0.765**	0.057	0.215
Broad organizational restructuring	0.157	**0.556**	-0.065	0.428
Unsatisfactory project performance or failures	0.210	0.006	**0.557**	0.202
Competition with other parts of the organization either for mandates or for resources	-0.001	0.160	**0.759**	0.004
Changes in the total project workload i.e., number, size or complexity of projects	0.152	-0.040	**0.743**	0.139
New PMO manager	0.072	0.011	0.166	**0.745**
New vision and/or strategy of the executive team	0.038	0.312	0.141	**0.650**
% VARIANCE	19.24	15.75	12.67	10.24
% AVERAGE CUMMULATIVE	19.24	34.99	47.66	57.90
CRONBACH ALPHA	0.787	0.712	0.552	0.386

Note. Factor loadings >.50 are in boldface.

7.1.1 Issues Related to a PMO Change

Four reliable factors were identified among the issues related to PMO changes, shown in Table 7.2. The first factor labeled *portfolio management and methods* contains four variables commonly related to multi-project management in general and to project portfolio management in particular. These four variables form a conceptually homogeneous group. The factor also contains the variable which fits between project management methods and project characteristics. The loading of this last variable is smaller than the others. However, there is an element of consistency. Portfolio management is associated with grouping projects by type. One of the uses of such typologies is to customize methods to the needs of each project type or to the project characteristics. Finally, the factor includes the variable on standardization of project management methods. Even if this element is rarely mentioned as part of project portfolio management standards, standardization is prerequisite to any aggregation of projects at portfolio level. One expected result showed that issues related to standardization are perceived by respondents as associated to portfolio management. Müller, Martinsuo and Blomquist

(2008) showed that the use of standardized reporting methods and metrics are a prerequisite for portfolio performance. This link between disciplined behavior across all projects in a portfolio and the portfolio's performance is reflected in the combination of variables that load on this factor.

The second factor is labeled *collaboration and accountability*. It contains four variables related to collaboration among project stakeholders. This factor summarizes the human relationship dimension of PMO work. All the variables loading on this factor relate to agency theory (Jensen, 2000). This theory addresses the problem of human interaction in the context of information and power imbalance. Central aspects of this theory are the two problems related to delegation of work:

- Was the work delegated to the right person? Does he or she have the skills and other abilities required to succeed?
- Will the person chosen for delegation act in the best interest of those who delegated the work?

Table 7.2. Factor Analysis of Issues Related to PMO Change

Survey Items	ISSUE 1 Portfolio Management and Methods	ISSUE 2 Collaboration and Accountability	ISSUE 3 Project Management Maturity and Performance	ISSUE 4 Work Climate
Project alignment with strategy	**0.678**	0.164	0.270	-0.139
Availability of relevant information to decision makers	**0.689**	0.371	0.171	0.131
Project selection	**0.740**	0.113	0.034	-0.045
Allocation of resources across multiple projects	**0.795**	0.173	-0.114	0.177
Fit between project management methods and project characteristics	**0.522**	-0.001	0.235	0.450
Standardization of project management methods	**0.661**	-0.038	0.452	0.218
Customer and stakeholder relations	0.097	**0.730**	0.078	0.091
Project management and line collaboration	0.113	**0.734**	0.073	0.160
Tensions or conflicts within the organization	0.096	**0.511**	-0.081	0.207
Accountability for projects	0.176	**0.707**	0.270	-0.017
Synergy among project managers	0.161	**0.594**	0.371	0.227
Organizational commitment to project management	0.029	0.299	**0.631**	-0.003
Project management skill level	0.086	0.183	**0.709**	0.381
Project performance	0.392	0.434	**0.539**	0.042
Project management maturity	0.487	0.107	**0.582**	0.099
Work climate	0.024	0.121	0.234	**0.714**
Work-family balance	0.112	0.259	0.044	**0.816**
% VARIANCE	18.53	15.56	12.24	10.01
% VARIANCE CUMMULATIVE	18.53	34.09	46.33	56.34
CRONBACH ALPHA	0.833	0.721	0.754	0.677

Note. Factor loadings >.50 are in boldface.

Agency problems occur whenever responsibility is delegated (for example, at every node of an organizational hierarchy or network, as well as at the point of interface between organizations, projects and stakeholders). Crawford, Cooke-Davies, Hobbs, Labuschagne, Remington, and Chen (2008) showed that being accountable for projects requires collaboration with a variety of key stakeholders. This research on project sponsorship gives an example of strong links between the sponsor, the project, and the permanent organization, including the PMO.

The third factor has been labeled *project management maturity and performance*. It encompasses the variables of organizational commitment to project management, project management skill level, project performance, and project management maturity. These form a consistent group of issues. The strongest weighting is on project management skill level. The association with maturity is intuitive. That organizational commitment to project management is associated with both is also intuitive, as both of these variables would be more of an issue in organizations where commitment to project management is also an issue. It is conceptually consistent that in situations where the other three variables are issues, project performance would also be an issue. These four variables, therefore, form a consistent set of issues.

The fourth factor has been labeled *work climate*. It contains two variables that are conceptually consistent and readily interpreted. These variables on work climate were added following interviews done in Sweden, as part of our case studies research (see section in Chapter Three). None of the Canadian interviewees mentioned this issue; interestingly, Turner and Müller (2006) met the same phenomenon when doing interviews in Sweden as part of their research on how to choose the right project manager for a project. Only Swedish managers of project managers said that the project manager's ability to successfully balance work and private life is a criterion for selecting a project manager for a project. This confirms that national cultural dimension may have to be taken into account when considering factors of PMO change.

Only two variables were left as orphans: *business performance* and *cost of PMO*. Both are unrelated to the other issues. It is particularly interesting that business performance is unrelated to any other issue. This suggests the question: what *is* related to business performance?

7.1.2 The Relative Importance of the Drivers

The internal and external events and issues all provide explanations of the forces driving the changes to the PMO. There are significant differences in the average importance of several of the drivers. Table 7.3 shows the drivers in decreasing order of importance.

Table 7.3. Relative Importance of Drivers of PMO Change

Drivers	Means	Standard Deviation
Project management maturity and performance (ISSUE 3)	5.811	1.930
Portfolio management and methods (ISSUE 1)	5.367	2.054
Collaboration and accountability (ISSUE 2)	5.338	1.763
Change in top management (EVENT 2)	4.127	2.220
Work climate (ISSUE 4)	3.682	2.196
External events (EVENT 1)	3.413	2.014

Project management maturity and performance is the most important driver. It is more important than Issue 1, portfolio management and methods ($p < 0.002$). Issues 1 and 2, collaboration and accountability, are of almost equal importance. Change in top management is significantly less important ($p < 0.000$), which is still more important than work climate ($p < 0.028$). Finally, external events are the least important and the difference with work climate is not particularly significant ($p < 0.05$).

7.2 The Nature of the Changes to PMOs

The analysis identified three reliable factors related to the nature of the change to the PMO (see Table 7.4). The first factor, labeled *PMO functions and supportiveness,* contains all nine PMO functions identified in this study plus the supportiveness of the PMO. Increases in the importance of all nine functions and increased supportiveness form a consistent factor.

The second factor, labeled *scope of control mandate,* contains increases in the controlling nature of the PMO, variables related to the scope of its mandate in terms of percentages of projects and project managers and higher hierarchical reporting level. Together they form a consistent image of increasing control and scope of mandate. Reporting to higher levels within the hierarchy is consistent with a wider mandate focused more on control.

The third factor, *PMO autonomy*, includes three variables. The first two variables form a consistent pair, associating more decision-making authority with more adequate funding for the PMO. The interpretation given here to the inclusion of the *PMO's lack of access to top management* is that a PMO with funds and decision-making authority should rarely require access to top management. This PMO is autonomous from both funding and decision-making perspectives.

Table 7.4. Factor Analysis of Changes to PMOs

Survey Items	CHANGE 1 PMO functions and Supportiveness	CHANGE 2 Scope of Control Mandate	CHANGE 3 PMO Autonomy
Monitor and control project performance, including the development of Projects Information System and the reporting function	**0.647**	0.349	0.380
Develop and implement standard methodologies, processes, and tools	**0.790**	0.138	0.214
Develop competency of project personnel including training and mentoring	**0.805**	0.005	0.230
Multi-project management, including program and portfolio management, coordination and allocation of resources between projects	**0.846**	0.105	0.187
Strategic management including participation in strategic planning and benefits management	**0.697**	-0.044	0.384
Organizational learning including the management of lessons learned, audits and monitoring of PMO performance	**0.805**	0.062	0.348
Management of customer interfaces	**0.718**	0.156	0.157
Recruit, select, evaluate and determine salaries for Project Managers	**0.679**	0.266	0.026
Execute specialized tasks for project managers, e.g., preparation of schedules	**0.723**	0.261	-0.211
Supportive	**0.672**	0.147	0.234
Controlling	0.322	**0.577**	0.065
Percentage of these projects within PMO's mandate	0.041	**0.758**	0.230
Percentage of project managers reporting to the PMO manager	0.040	**0.784**	0.145
The hierarchical level to which the PMO reports is:	0.179	**0.557**	0.439
The PMO's lack of access to top management (note inverted scale)	0.197	0.130	**0.784**
Level of the PMO's decision-making authority	0.297	0.398	**0.639**
Funding for the PMO	0.203	0.360	**0.670**
% VARIANCE	34.10	14.59	14.20
% VARIANCE CUMMULATIVE	34.10	48.69	62.89
CRONBACH ALPHA	0.929	0.717	0.767

Note. Factor loadings >.50 are in boldface.

The analysis excluded three orphan variables from the factors: *extent of organizational culture's support for the PMO, PMO's accountability for project performance (Scope, costs & schedule)*, and *PMO's accountability for project performance (Benefits)*.

7.3 Impact After the Change

The list of variables to assess the impact of PMO change are the same as the ones considered as issues for change. For each item, the questionnaire asked first for the importance of each reason for change and then for the impact after the change. The objective of this approach is to assess whether the PMO change has some impact on the initial issues. The factor analysis of impacts identified three reliable impact factors (see Table 7.5).

Table 7.5. Factor Analysis of Impacts of Changes to PMOs

Survey Items	IMPACT 1 Portfolio Management and Methods	IMPACT 2 Collaboration, Accountability and Skills	IMPACT 3 Work Climate and Cost of PMO
Project alignment with strategy	0.766	0.429	0.110
Availability of relevant information to decision makers	0.792	0.337	0.056
Project selection	0.812	0.037	0.180
Allocation of resources across multiple projects	0.724	0.269	0.285
Fit between project management methods and project characteristics	0.691	0.380	0.237
Organizational commitment to project management	0.269	0.797	0.033
Customer and stakeholder relations	0.004	0.634	0.373
Project management and line collaboration	0.212	0.807	0.013
Accountability for projects	0.324	0.705	0.165
Synergy among project managers	0.407	0.572	0.122
Project management skill level	0.444	0.611	0.267
Work climate	0.437	0.377	0.545
Work-family balance	0.295	0.100	0.781
Cost of PMO	0.065	0.085	0.749
% VARIANCE	26.73	25.45	13.62
% VARIANCE CUMMULATIVE	26.73	52.17	65.80
CRONBACH ALPHA	0.893	0.864	0.675

Note. Factor loadings >.50 are in boldface.

The issue factors and the impact factors show both similarities and differences. The issue and impact factors are compared and contrasted in Table 7.6. The first element of difference is the number of factors: four factors on the issue side and three on the impact side. Globally, the factor analysis of impacts put aside four variables and added one variable to form three factors.

Two of the impact factors draw all of their variables from one issue factor. The correspondence between these issue and impact factors is obvious. The impact factor *collaboration, accountability and skills* consists of a selection of variables from two issue factors. The issue and impact factors are compared and contrasted in the following paragraphs.

Table 7.6. Comparison between Issues and Impact Factors

Issue Factors	Variables	Impact Factors
1. Portfolio management and methods	Project alignment with strategy	1. Portfolio and methods
	Standardization of project management methods	
	Availability of relevant information to decision makers	
	Project selection	
	Allocation of resources across multiple projects	
	Fit between project management methods and project characteristics	
	Standardization of project management methods	
2. Collaboration and accountability	Tensions or conflicts within the organization	
	Customer and stakeholder relations	2. Collaboration, accountability, and skills
	Accountability for projects	
	Synergy among project managers	
	Project management and line collaboration	
2. Project management maturity and performance	Organizational commitment to project management	
	Project management skill level	
	Project performance	
	Project management maturity	
3. Work Climate	Work climate	3. Work climate and cost of PMO
	Work-family equilibrium	
	Cost of PMO	

The *portfolio management and methods* factor includes the same variables on both sides, except for the variable standardization of project management methods that is excluded from the impact factor. Its removal, therefore, creates a factor that is conceptually consistent and very similar.

The second factor on both sides relates to collaboration and accountability, but significant differences exist on variables included or not on each side. On the impact side, this factor does not include the variable on tensions and conflicts. But it includes two variables on commitment and skills in project management. The impact factor *collaboration, accountability and skills* brings together the variables related to the human side of project management, excluding the darker elements related to tensions and conflicts. Conceptually, the issue and impact factors related to collaboration and accountability are quite similar.

Two variables have been excluded from the factor analysis on the impact side: *project performance* and *project management maturity*. These two variables could be classified as part of an issue leading to PMO change, but they are not included in any impact factors from this change.

The *work climate* factor on the issue side also forms a third factor on the impact side with an additional variable, that of the cost of the PMO. In the current literature, cost of a PMO is rarely associated with work climate (Kendal

& Rollins, 2003). One example which contrasts this can be found in Miranda (2003). The logic behind this factor relates to the social costs of not respecting equilibrium between family and work. The work climate plays a similar role. The PMO is seen as a locus of coordination for the total individual workload and has a mandate for balancing efforts. Consequences could be lack of quality, absenteeism, burnout and sickness, all of them generating costs for the PMO through rework, activities for recruitment and diminishing productivity. Likewise, pressures to improve productivity and control costs may contribute to the deterioration of the work-family equilibrium and the work climate.

7.4 Correlations Among Factors

The factor analysis has reduced the number of variables considerably. The analysis has identified two event factors, four issue factors, three PMO change factors and three impact factors. The next step in the analysis is to investigate the relationships among these factors using correlation analysis.

The factor correlation matrix is shown in Appendix F, which also shows the Pearson correlation coefficient and the two-tailed significance test. Correlation coefficients above 0.34 are highlighted. In interpreting the correlations, it should be remembered that the percentage of variance explained is equal to the square of the Pearson coefficient. A coefficient of 0.34 thus explains 10% of the variance and a coefficient of 0.20 explains only 4%. The result may be statistically different from zero but still may not be meaningful in terms of guiding management action.

Overall, there is very little correlation among the factors. Because the Varimax method was used, there are no correlations within each set of factors. There are six correlation coefficients greater than 0.34, of which only one is greater than 0.5. Three of these show a relationship between the issue and the impact factors. When an issue drives a change through a PMO, improvement tends to be observed in this issue. For example, the strongest correlation is between the portfolio management and method issue and improvement on these same issues as shown by the impact factor. The same is true for the issues of collaboration and accountability and of work climate. An obvious result such as this is reassuring that it confirms the reliability of the data.

The three other correlation coefficients are between 0.34 and 0.40. These are noteworthy but not particularly strong correlations. The first condition factor, conditions external to the organization, is related to two other factors, issues related to work climate and impacts on collaboration, accountability, and skill. The interpretation of the first relationship is quite straightforward. The external conditions are all related to increasing pressure on the organization. As can be observed in most organizations, this increased pressure has repercussions for the work climate and for the work-family equilibrium, as more pressure is put on employees to meet increasing demands.

The relationship between external conditions and the collaboration, accountability and skills factor mirrors the correlations between external conditions and people's attitudes as a reaction to these conditions. When looking at the variables that make up these factors, it is evident that the external factors relate to changes in economy, industry, markets, political systems, regulations, social responsibilities and ethics. They comprise hard factors (such as regulations) but also softer factors (such as ethics) which could be hypothesized to impact behavior and the psychological contracts people have with their customers, suppliers, employer, and colleagues.

The factor on collaboration, accountability and skills reflects this hypothesis. It summarizes the variables on commitment and relationships, plus the willingness (or freedom) to take on accountability for improving skills in a changing external environment. The positive correlation between the two factors shows an increase in the willingness (or freedom) to take on accountability, collaborate with stakeholders and colleagues and increase one's skills in the case of increasing turbulence in the external environment. PMO changes undertaken following changes in the external conditions should benefit the management of projects as collaboration, accountability and skills are directly linked to behavioral success factors (Slevin & Pinto, 2004). Interestingly, changes in the internal conditions did not relate to this impact on collaboration, accountability and skills.

The only other correlation coefficient greater than 0.34 is found between increases in the importance of the functions filled by the PMO and the supportiveness of the PMO, which are both related to improvements in portfolio management and methods. Many of the PMO functions are related to project management methods and this impact factor is also related to methods. This may explain, at least partially, why they are associated.

Figure 7.1 illustrates the six relationships among factors from the correlation analysis. The general lack of relationships among the factors, other than the obvious ones between issues and impacts, is one of the major results of this study. No correlation between the conditions and issues that drive changes through PMO and the changes that are made within the PMOs were identified. No pattern was found in which certain conditions drive certain types of changes to PMOs, which in turn produce certain organizational impacts. There was however, one type of change to PMOs that leads to a particular impact: increases in the importance of PMO functions and supportiveness is associated with improvements in portfolio management and methods.

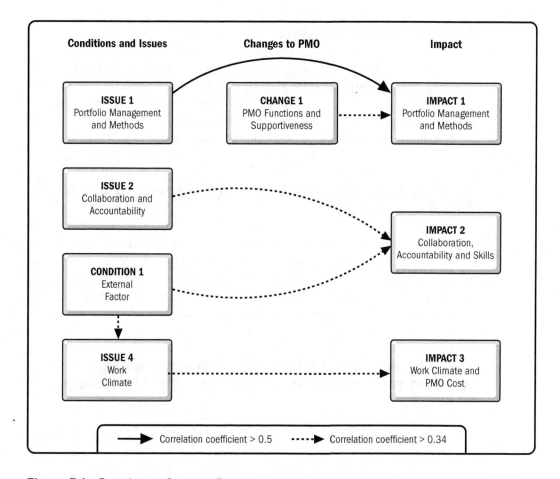

Figure 7.1. Correlations Between Factors

7.5 Correlations With Contextual Factors

The drivers of change, the changes to the PMO and the impacts of the changes may be more or less significant in different contexts. These relationships are explored in this section using correlation analysis. Only significant correlations ($p < 0.05$) are reported.

7.5.1 Contextual Factors

Three contextual factors were correlated significantly with events, issues, PMO changes and impact factors. These are organization size, level of project management maturity and presence of internal project customers. All the associations were positive.

7.5.2 Implementation

Three aspects of the implementation of the changes to the PMOs were shown to vary with different issues, changes and impacts. These are ease of implementation, speed of implementation and the use of change management practices. All associations were positive. No factors were associated with easier or faster implementation or with lack of use of change management.

7.5.3 Associations With the Importance of External Events (Event 1)

The use of change management is the only contextual variable associated with the importance of external events as drivers of change. When external events are driving the change, the implementation is seen more often as an important organizational change and is managed as such. Event 2, top management change, was not associated with any of the contextual variables.

7.5.4 Associations With the Importance of Issues Related to Portfolio Management and Methods (Issue 1)

As would be expected, issues related to portfolio management and methods are more salient in large organizations that conduct projects for internal customers. Obvious results are reassuring in that they show the data is reliable. Change management is also used more often in this context. Changes to portfolio management and methods involve many internal stakeholders and require that many employees adhere to the changes. The use of change management practices is particularly relevant in such contexts.

7.5.5 Associations With the Importance of Issues Related to Collaboration and Accountability (Issue 2)

Changes to PMOs that are made in response to issues related to collaboration and accountability are more difficult to implement. These issues are clearly related to human and political aspects of the organization and require the involvement and adhesion of employees. The use of change management would be indicated but the results show that change management is not used more or less often on these types of change efforts.

7.5.6 Associations With the Importance of Issues Related to Project Management Maturity and Performance (Issue 3)

Interestingly, issues related to project management maturity and performance are more salient in mature organizations. It would seem that mature organizations focus more on project management practices and performance. This does not mean that they perform more poorly, only that performance is a more salient issue. It would seem that more mature organizations are more likely to undertake changes to improve their project management processes and performance. This may be a reflection of the higher levels of maturity associated with continuous improvement.

7.5.7 Associations with Increases in the Functions Filled By the PMO and Its Supportiveness (Change 1)

Augmenting the role of the PMO by increasing the number of functions it fills, the extent to which it fills various project management functions or its supportiveness, as is shown by the correlation with the length of time the change takes to implement.

7.5.8 Associations With Increases in the Scope and the Controlling Nature of the PMO's Mandate (Change 2)

Increasing the scope of the PMO's mandate and giving it more of a controlling role is an organizational change that is both long and difficult to implement. Organizations implementing this change do not use change management any more or any less. Given that these changes are long and difficult, it would seem that organizations implementing such changes would be advised to use change management practices. No contextual variables were associated with increases in the autonomy of the PMO (Change 3).

7.5.9 Associations With Improvements in Portfolio Management and Methods (Impact 1)

Improvements in portfolio management and methods take longer to implement but organizations implementing such changes use change management more often. This is consistent with the fact that organizations that initiate changes to their PMO driven by these issues use change management more often.

7.5.10 Associations With Improvements in Collaboration, Accountability and Skill (Impact 2)

Improvements in collaboration, accountability and skill imply changes to the social tissue of organizations. Organizations that show improvements in these issues use change management more often, which is not surprising. No contextual variables are associated with Impact 3, improvements in work climate and cost of PMO.

7.6 Key Findings

The key findings in this chapter are as follows:
1. The case studies identified a large number of reasons for PMO changes, changes that are made to PMOs and impacts of these changes. The descriptive statistics presented in Chapter Five showed that most or all of these variables were important. It is difficult to draw conclusions from the variety of information presented in Chapter Five. The factor analysis identified underlying patterns that reduced this great variety to a small number of factors for each of these groups of variables.
2. All five of the external contextual variables were grouped into one factor with no variables excluded from the analysis. All of the variables related to changes in the economic and/or institutional context.
3. The changes in the economic and institutional context were shown to have a weak impact on the importance of issues related to the working climate and to equilibrium between family and work. Presumably this is because the increasing demands put upon the organization are producing greater demands on employees and bringing demands from the workplace into conflict with family life.
4. Change in top management was the only factor that was identified that related to events and conditions within the organization. Change in top management was also related to broad organizational change. The several examples of changes in top management were all related, indicating that such changes tend not to be isolated events but to form a pattern of general structural change in the organization.
5. The qualitative case studies identified five other organizational conditions that can provoke changes to PMOs. These are: new PMO manager, new vision and/ or strategy of the executive team, unsatisfactory project performance or failure, competition for mandates or resources and changes in the workload. None of these factors were related to changes in top management, meaning that they exist independently from such changes. Because they do not form a reliable factor, they were not measured in these analyses. The qualitative case studies and the scores for the importance of each of these organizational conditions showed that they are, however, part of the explanation of why PMOs change.
6. Many issues can drive changes to PMOs. The factor analysis found an underlying structure of four factors: portfolio management and methods,

collaboration and accountability, project management maturity and performance, and work climate.

7. Only two issues were not included in the issue factors: business performance and the cost of the PMO. It is interesting that these two issues are unrelated to the other issues. This leads the authors to question to what, exactly, these two issues may relate. The lack of a relationship between issues of business performance and other issues is particularly intriguing in the light of the current interest in the contribution of project management to business performance (Thomas & Mullaly, 2008). Are project management issues unrelated to business performance?

8. PMOs are complex entities. Changing a PMO can mean changing many different things. The factor analysis identified an underlying structure of four different types of changes made to PMOs. The most important were changes to the roles or functions filled by the PMO. The analysis was quite efficient in that it only excluded two design variables: accountability for scope, costs and schedule and for benefits. It would seem that despite the great number of possible changes that can be made to PMOs, there is an underlying pattern among the organizational choices being made that reduces these choices considerably.

9. Changes to PMOs produce impacts on the organization. These impacts were evaluated in this study by the degree of improvement or deterioration in the issues that are related to changes in PMOs. Not surprisingly, when a PMO is changed because of an issue, there is a tendency to find an improvement in that issue. As expected, there was considerable similarity between the results of the factor analyses of issues and of impacts. Beyond this rather obvious conclusion, the analysis of the impacts of change provided few insights.

10. The analysis failed to reveal a pattern among the factors. Conditions and issues driving changes to PMO were generally not related to the actual changes made to the PMOs. Organizational reality is plausibly too complex and too subtle to reveal simple relationships whereby a particular condition or issue would lead to a particular change in the PMO. The next chapter explores the data in search of more complex mediating and moderating effects.

11. The examination of associations between contextual variables and the issues, changes and impacts associated with PMO transitions did not identify many significant patterns. There were only two significant findings. First, large organizations doing projects for internal customers see portfolio management and methods as more important issues, which is an intuitive result. Second, more mature organizations see maturity and performance as more important issues. This is somewhat surprising at first glance, but it is consistent with a mature process for continuous improvement.

12. Several associations were identified between the process for implementing changes to PMOs and the drivers of change, the nature of the changes being implemented and the improvements that were delivered. This highlights the importance of questions related to implementation and the variability found among organizations in this regard.

CHAPTER EIGHT: SURVEY RESULTS: MEDIATING AND MODERATING EFFECTS

This chapter aims to identify more subtle patterns among the factors identified in Chapter Seven and with the organizational context. Two types of analyses are presented.

First, analyses are presented that explore possible mediating effects. Such effects take the form presented in Figure 8.1, where A has an impact on B which in turn has an impact on C. B is said to have a mediating effect on the relationship between A and C.

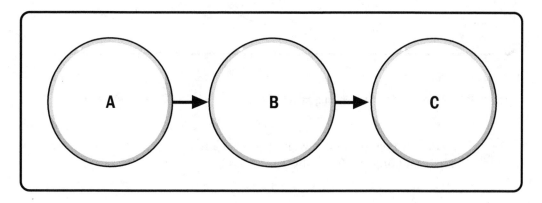

Figure 8.1. Model of the Mediating Effect of B in the Relation Between A and C

Next, analyses are presented that explore possible moderating effects as shown in Figure 8.2 where B has an impact on the relation between A and C. B is said to have a moderating effect on the relation between A and C.

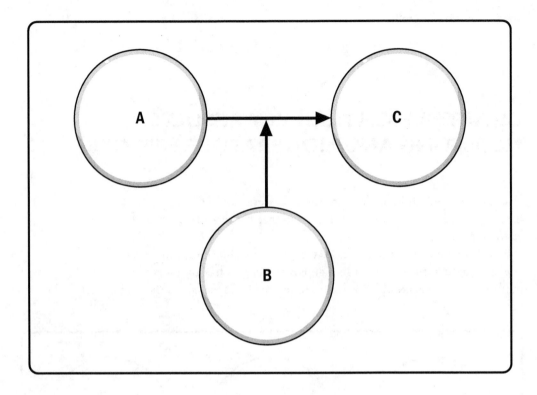

Figure 8.2. Model of the Moderating Effect of B on the Relation Between A and C

The chapter concludes with an overall discussion of these two groups of analyses and presents key findings.

8.1 Mediating Effects

Correlation coefficients identify that a relation exists between two variables, but do not indicate which is the independent and the dependent variable. The logical relationship among the variables in Figure 2.2 and the way questions were formulated in the survey instrument clearly indicate that Event and Issue factors drive changes to the PMO, which in turn produced Impacts. Therefore, Impact factors always occupy the final C position or dependent variable in the relationship. Event and Issue factors are typically in the independent or A position except when more than one of these variables is present in the relation, in which case one will be in the independent or A position and the other in the mediating of B position. The contextual variables cannot be dependent variables, but could be either independent or mediating variables.

The correlations among the Event, Issue, Change and Impact factors identified in Chapter Seven and several contextual factors were examined to identify groups of three variables for which the following conditions exist as presented in Table 8.1 (see also Figure 8.1).

Table 8.1. Three Necessary Conditions for Mediating Effects

1	A is correlated with B
2	B is correlated with C
3	A is correlated with C

Note: Only correlations with a level of significance of $p < 0.05$ are considered in this analysis. These conditions are necessary but not sufficient.

In order for a mediating relation to exist, the standardized beta for B in the regression of the form $C = f(A, B)$ must be significant. If not, there is no mediating effect. If B is significant and A is not significant, B is a pure mediator. This means that the partial correlation of A with C when controlling for B is not significant. In other words, the effect of A on C is entirely due to the effect of A on B. If B is significant and the A is significant, B is a partial mediator, meaning that A has a direct effect on C and an indirect effect through B. For detailed information on the method employed see Kenny (2009).

8.1.1 Variables Mediating the Relationship Between External Events and Impact 2, Improvements in Collaboration, Accountability and Skill

A large number of possible groups of variables were identified and tested for these conditions. Only five groups of variables showed significant mediating effects, and of these, three showed effects mediating the effect of External Events on Improvements in Collaboration, Accountability and Skill. As was shown in Chapter 7, one of the strongest correlations is between these two factors. Given that the relationship between the independent and the dependent variables is relatively strong, it is not surprising that the three mediating effects identified by the analysis are partial, meaning that the direct effect of External Events remains and explains a significant amount of the improvement in the Impact on Collaboration, Accountability and Skill. In fact, the direct effect is stronger than the mediating effects. The direct and mediating effects are shown in Figure 8.3.

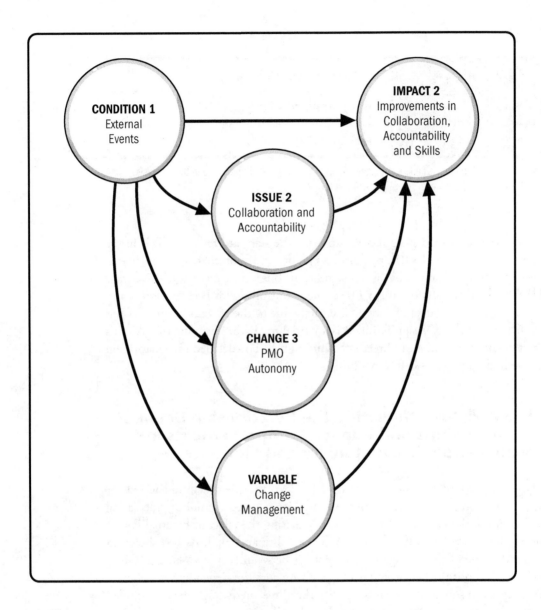

Figure 8.3. Partial Mediation of the Impact of External Events on Improvements in Collaboration, Accountability and Skills

External Events have an impact on the presence of Issue 2 related to collaboration and accountability, which was seen in Chapter Seven to be highly correlated with improvements in this issue (Impact 2). The relation between the importance of an issue in the decision to change the PMO and improvements to this same issue is common sense and almost tautological. It is understandable that pressures generated by events in the external economic and social environment lead to increasing salience of issues related to collaboration and accountability. This mediating effect is, therefore, conceptually consistent. This relationship is shown in the first mediating effect in Figure 8.3.

This relationship between External Events and Improvements in collaboration, accountability and skills is also mediated by increases in the autonomy of the PMO (Change 3), as shown by the second mediating relationship in Figure 8.3. In response to increased pressure from the environment, organizations have a tendency to give more autonomy to the PMO, which in turn leads to Improvements in collaboration, accountability and skills. This is one of the few examples found of a relation between the context and the changes made to the PMO.

The use of change management practices also has a mediating effect on the relationship between External Events and Improvements in collaboration, accountability and skills. It is not surprising that change management would have such an impact on organizational improvements in collaboration and accountability. This relationship is shown in the lower part of Figure 8.3.

8.1.2 Other Mediating Effects of Change Management

In addition to the mediating effect of change management presented above, change management was also shown to be part of one other significant mediating effect. The mediating effect of change management on the relation between Issue 4, Work climate, and Impact 2, collaboration, accountability and skills is shown in Figure 8.4. This is a pure mediating effect, meaning that when the mediating effect of change management is controlled for, the direct effect of Issue 4 on Impact 2 is not significant. This means that in the absence of change management practices the importance of Issue 4 has no effect on Impact 2.

However, in the presence of change management practices, the importance of work climate issues is related to Improvements in collaboration, accountability, and skills. All three variables in this mediation model are concerned with human relations. If work climate issues are important and change management practices are put in place, improvements in collaboration, accountability and skill will be greater. The results presented in Chapter Seven show that Improvements in collaboration, accountability and skills (Impact 2) are the most difficult to attain. The mediating effect of change management in cases where work climate is an important issue would produce greater improvements in Impact 2, which is a very consistent result.

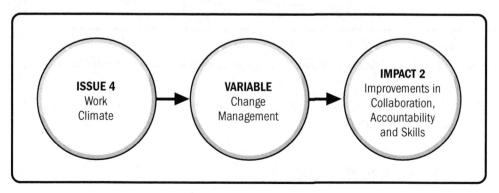

Figure 8.4. Pure Mediating Effect of Change Management

8.1.3 Mediation of the Relationship Between the Importance of Collaboration Issues and Accountability Issues (Issue 2) and Improvements in these Issues (Impact 2)

The final mediating effect identified is the partial mediating effect of changes to the scope and controlling nature of the PMO's mandate on the strong relationship between the importance of collaboration and accountability and improvements in these issues, as shown in Figure 8.5. This is one of the best indications of a pattern between the drivers of changes to PMOs, the changes made to PMOs, and the impacts of these changes. Organizations in which collaboration and accountability are important issues tend to implement changes that improve these issues. This is intuitive. If the organization increases the scope of the mandate of their PMO and gives it a more controlling role, improvements in collaboration, accountability and skill tend to be greater. That a more controlling PMO leads to improvements in accountability is intuitively reasonable. That a more controlling PMO is associated with improvements in collaboration is less intuitive.

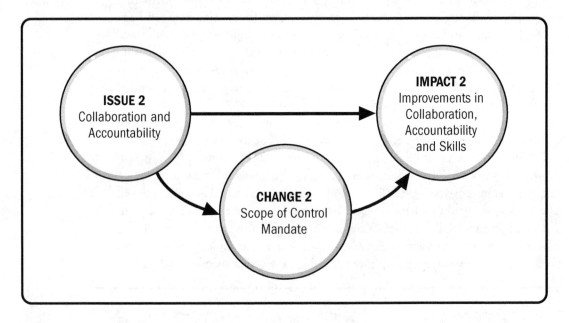

Figure 8.5. The Partial Mediation Effect of Increasing the Scope and Controlling Nature of the PMO's Mandate

The analysis of both mediating and moderating effects are discussed in the final sections of this chapter.

8.2 Moderating Effects

The general model of moderating effects was presented in Figure 8.2. There are two types of moderating effects: pure moderation and quasi-moderation.

Figure 8.2 presents a pure moderating effect in which the moderating variable does not have a direct effect on the dependant variable. The effect of the moderating variable is only on the relationship between A and C. The interpretation of a pure moderating effect is quite straightforward. In quasi-moderation, B also has a direct effect on C as shown in Figure 8.6. The effect of B is more complex and more difficult to interpret. Only two quasi-moderator effects were identified. All the others were identified as pure moderator effects.

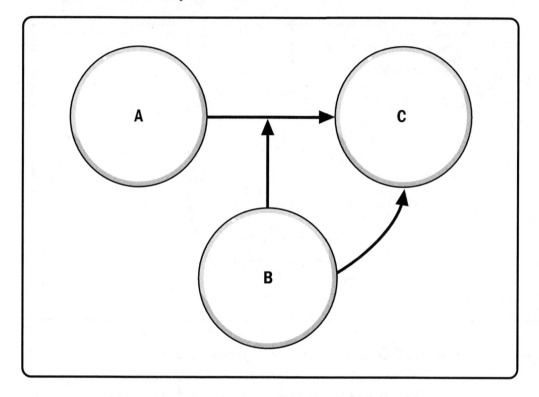

Figure 8.6. Illustration of the Quasi-Moderating Effect

Moderating effects can exist whether or not there is a significant relation between A and C. If a significant relation exists between A and C, then B affects the strength of this relation. If a significant relation does not exist between A and C, then B has an effect on the nature of the relation between A and B. For example, the relation between A and C may be positive for small values of B and negative for high values of B, or the relation between A and C may be significant for some values of B and not significant for others. The interpretation is quite straightforward once the nature of the effect is known.

Figure 8.7 presents a detailed model of the moderating effects that were investigated. Pure and quasi-moderator effects were identified using hierarchical regressions. The three dependent variables have been used as a basis for grouping the results of the analysis for presentation and interpretation.

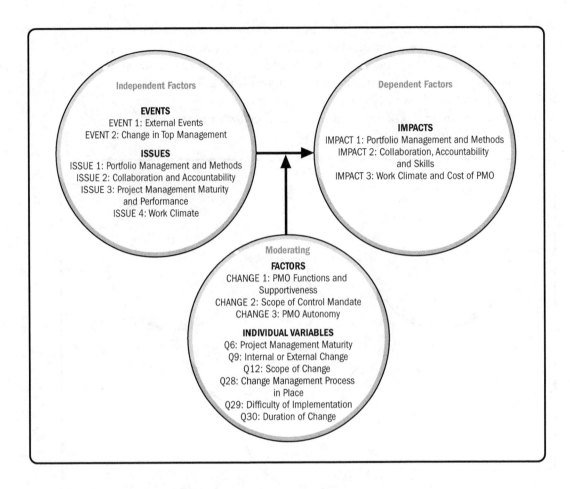

Figure 8.7. Research Model for the Identification of Moderator Variables

8.2.1 Moderating Effects on Impact 1: Improvements in Portfolio Management and Methods

Three variables were found to have moderating effects on Impact 1, Improvements in portfolio management and methods. The results presented in Chapter Seven showed a strong correlation between the importance of Issue 1 related to portfolio management and methods and improvements on these issues. This relationship is moderated by changes to the scope of the PMO's mandate and to increases in the control it exerts (Change 2), as shown in Figure 8.8. The effect is negative, meaning that the greater the increases in the scope of the PMO's mandate and the controlling nature of its role, the smaller the improvements in issues related to portfolio management and methods. This is a pure moderating effect, meaning that these changes to the PMO's mandate have no direct effect on improvements to portfolio management and methods. The moderating effect is much smaller than the direct effect but this does give an indication that organizations that change the mandate of the PMO in this way generate less improvement in portfolio management and methods.

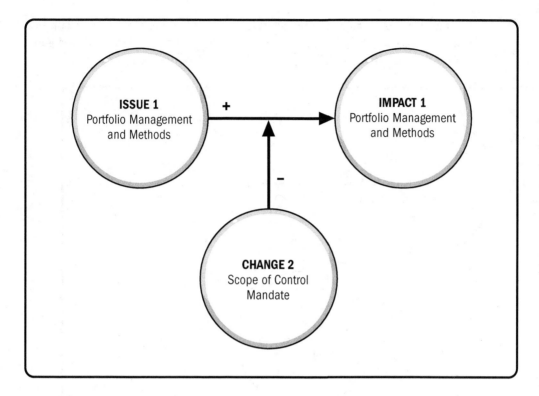

Figure 8.8. The Negative Pure Moderating Effect of Increase in the Scope of Control of the PMO's Mandate

Moderating effects were also identified for the relationships between the independent variables external events (Event 1) and top management change (Event 2) and the improvements in portfolio management and methods (Impact 1). In both cases, no significant relationship existed in the absence of the moderating effect. In addition, both moderating effects are quasi-moderating effects as shown in Figure 8.6, meaning that the moderating variables also have a direct effect on improvements in portfolio management and methods.

The relationship between changes in top management (Event 2) and the improvements in portfolio management and methods (Impact 1) is moderated by increases in the importance of the functions the PMO fills in the organization and the supportiveness of its role (Change 1), as shown in Figure 8.9. For small changes to the PMO, the effect of the importance of changes to top management is associated with deterioration in portfolio management and methods. For larger changes in Change 1, changes in top management are not associated with changes in portfolio management and methods. In other words, if changes in top management are not an important driver of PMO change, the effect of increasing the PMO's functions and supportiveness is deterioration in portfolio management and methods. This moderating effect is small and is overshadowed by the direct effect of increases in the importance of the functions the PMO fills in the organization and the supportiveness of its role (Change 1) on portfolio management and methods, shown in Chapter Seven and Figure 7.1 (p < 0.001). The direct effect and the moderating effect of

Change 1 are opposites. The moderating effect adds some contextual detail, but is not strong enough to impact the general findings of the analysis. This is a good example of the difficulty in interpreting quasi-moderator effects.

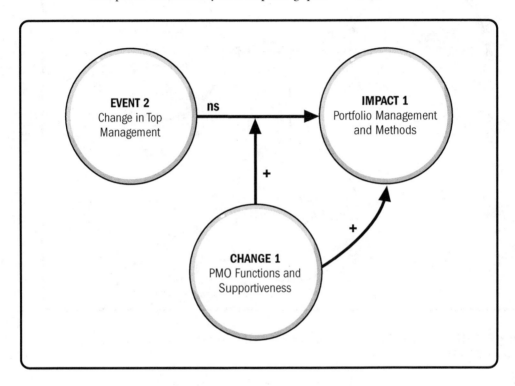

Figure 8.9. The Quasi-Moderating Effect of Increases in the Functions Filled by the PMO and its Supportiveness

The relationship between External Events (Event 1) and Improvements in portfolio management and methods (Impact 1) is also moderated by the length of time it takes to implement the change to the PMO, as shown in Figure 8.10. If the change is rapid, the importance of external events has a negative effect on portfolio management and methods. If change is slow, no effect was observed. This is consistent with the correlation between the length of time taken to implement the change and improvements in portfolio management and methods.

In other words, a slow implementation leads to greater improvements in portfolio management and methods than a quick implementation and with a slow implementation there is no moderating effect of Event 1. With fast implementations, the improvements in portfolio management and methods are smaller, and in the presence of external events as important drivers of change, the changes in portfolio management and methods show less improvement or deterioration. As was shown in section 7.5.9, improvements to portfolio management and methods take longer to implement, on average, than other changes, and organizations use change management practices during the implementation. In the presence of important External Events, faster implementation has greater negative effects. The moderating and direct effects are therefore mutually reinforcing and consistent.

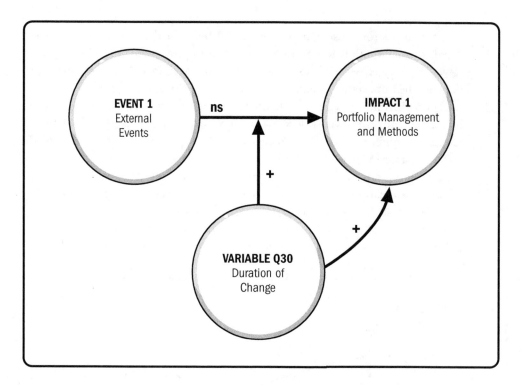

Figure 8.10. The Quasi-Moderator Effect of Speed of Implementation

However, both the moderating effect and the direct effect explain small percentages of the variance in improvements in portfolio management and methods. These two were the only quasi-moderating effects that were identified. All other effects were identified as pure moderating effects, which are simpler to interpret.

The pure moderating effect of Change 2 on the relationship between Issue 1 and Impact 1 and the quasi-moderating effect of Change 1 on the relationship between Event 2 and Impact 1 both give indications of the effects of specific changes to PMOs and their impact on portfolio management and methods. These are among the most important results, as they indicate that a pattern might exist between drivers of PMO change, changes to PMOs, and their impacts.

8.2.2 Moderating Effects on Impact 2: Improvements in Collaboration, Accountability and Skill

Five moderating effects on Impact 2 were found, in three of which the level of project management maturity is the moderating variable. In two of these three cases, the moderating effect was positive, but in the third it was negative. Maturity positively moderates the importance of issues related to portfolio management and methods (Issue 1) and the importance of issues related to collaboration and accountability (Issue 2) on Impact 2. Maturity negatively moderates the effects of external events (Event 1). These are all pure moderating effects, meaning that project management maturity does not have a direct effect on improvements in collaboration, accountability, and skill.

There is a strong association (p < 0.000) between the importance of issues related to collaboration and accountability and improvements in these issues, as shown in Chapter Seven. This association is stronger in mature organizations. Likewise, the importance of external events as drivers of PMO change (Event 1) is associated with improvements in collaboration, accountability and skills (p < 0.007). The relationship is, however, weaker in more mature organizations. In general, there is no significant relationship between the importance of issues related to portfolio management and methods (Issue 1) and improvements in collaboration, accountability and skill (Impact 2), but in high-maturity organizations there is a positive association. The moderating effect of project management maturity is therefore mixed. In two cases it led to greater improvements in collaboration, accountability and skill, while in one case it had the opposite effect. The three moderator effects of project management maturity are shown in Figure 8.11.

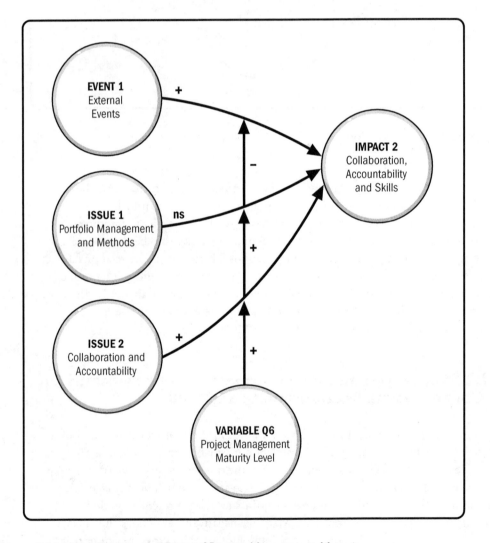

Figure 8.11. Pure Moderator Effects of Project Management Maturity

Project management maturity has a moderating effect on the relationship between issues related to collaboration and accountability and improvements.. This moderating effect means that mature organizations that change their PMO with the aim of making improvements in these issues produce greater improvements than less mature organizations. Note, however, that there is no direct effect of project management maturity on improvements in these issues. This means that only when these issues are the drivers of change do mature organizations make greater improvements. This could be interpreted to mean that when issues related to collaboration and accountability have been identified as important, mature organizations are better able to identify and implement the changes that will lead to improvements in these issues.

In the literature and in practice, project management maturity is associated with the ability to use project management methods more systematically and hopefully to deliver better project performance. The moderating effect discussed here indicates that there may be other competencies associated with project management maturity; in this case, the ability to make improvement when faced with certain issues. Higher levels of maturity include the monitoring of processes and their continuous improvement, which is consistent with the moderating effect identified here. This is a more dynamic conception of project management maturity than that found in the current literature.

The two other moderating effects of maturity can also be interpreted to gain some insights into the nature of more mature and less mature organizations. However, these other interpretations are more speculative, because they do not relate to improvements that were the express aim of the change. When issues related to portfolio management are driving a change to a PMO, organizations generally implement changes that lead to improvements in these issues. However, more mature organizations also make improvements in collaboration, accountability and methods. Less mature organizations do not. This may be a more subtle indication of a greater ability to make improvements in more mature organizations.

The fact that more mature organizations make less improvement in collaboration, accountability and methods when external changes are driving the PMO change may indicate that mature organizations are more focused on internal processes than less mature organizations. The three moderating effects of project management maturity can thus generate some new hypotheses about the ability of organizations with mature project management processes to manage change in their PMOs.

Two other moderating effects were identified for improvements in collaboration, accountability and skills. There is a weak association between the importance of issues related to work climate and improvements in collaboration, accountability and skill ($p < 0.066$). Organizations that have these issues tend to bring about changes that result in such improvements. Both are based on human relations. This relationship is reinforced by the difficulty in implementing the change. In other words, in contexts where the changes are more difficult to implement, the association between work climate issues and improvements in collaboration, accountability, and skills are stronger. However, the effects here are quite small.

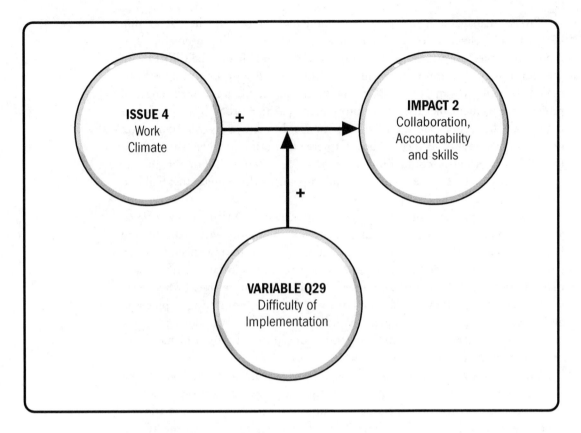

Figure 8.12. Pure Moderator Effect of Difficulty of Implementation

The importance of issues related to project management maturity and performance (Issue 3) are weakly associated with improvements in collaboration, accountability and skill ($p < 0.017$). When the autonomy of the PMO is increased (Change 3), the association is weaker. This is a pure moderating effect, meaning that Change 3 has no direct effect of Impact 2, but decreases the association between Issue 3 and Impact 2. This relation is illustrated in Figure 8.13. Because the effects are small and the relation indirect, this result contributes little to an understanding of the dynamics of PMO transformations.

8.2.3 Moderating Effects on Impact 3: Work Climate and Cost of PMO

Four moderating variables were found to have a moderating effect on relations with Impact 3. As shown in Chapter Seven, a significant association ($p < 0.000$) exists between the importance of issues related to work climate (Issue 4) and improvements in these issues (Impact 3). This association is moderated by change management practices. It is not surprising to find that change management practices increase the effectiveness of changes put in place to improve work climate as both relate strongly to human issues.

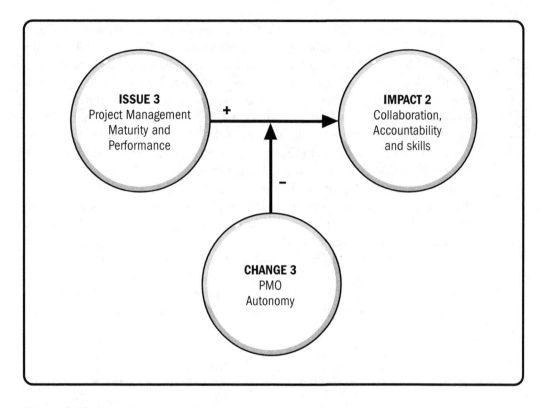

Figure 8.13. Pure Moderator Effect of Increases in PMO Autonomy

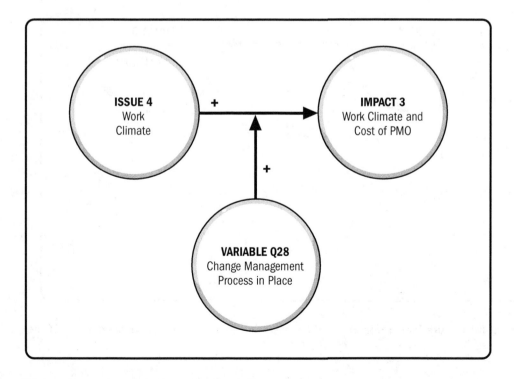

Figure 8.14. Pure Moderator Effect of Change Management

Three other models were identified in which there exists no significant relationship between the independent variable and Impact 3 when the relationship is not moderated. When the PMO mandate is changed significantly to increase the functions it fills and the supportiveness of its role (Change 1), external events (Event 1) have been shown to have a positive association with improvements in work climate and cost of PMO (Impact 3), but only for large changes in the PMO. When small changes of this type are made to the PMO, no association exists. The correlation results presented in Chapter Seven show that Event 1 is associated with issues (p < 0.000) related to work climate (Issue 4), which in turn is associated with improvements in Impact 3 (p < 0.000). As was argued in Chapter Seven, External Events may put pressure on the people in the organization and have the effect of deteriorating the work climate. The correlation between Event 1 and Impact 3 is not significant (p < 0.127). However, for high values of Change 1, the association is significant. This is an indication that this specific change to PMOs has an impact on the association between external events and improvements in work climate and PMO cost. This is an example of a pattern in the relationships between drivers of PMO change, the changes that are put in place, and the impact of these changes.

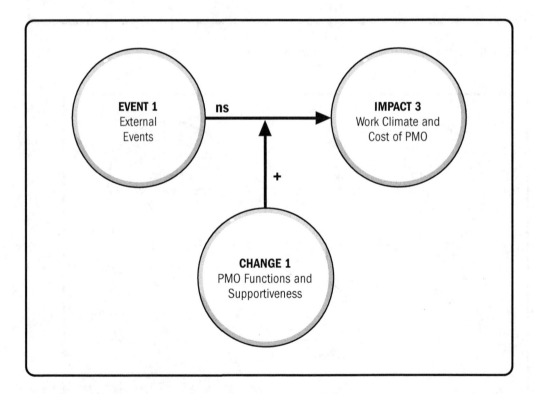

Figure 8.15. Pure Moderator Effect of Increases in the Functions and Supportiveness of the PMO

Change in top management (Event 2) has been shown to be associated with improvements in work climate and PMO cost for organizations that do projects for external customers, but not for organizations that do projects for internal customers. It is possible that organizations that do projects for internal customers have a more complex political environment with more internal players. It would seem that changes in top management in this more complex political environment lead as often to improvements to the working climate and perceptions of the value of the PMO as they lead to deterioration. In organizations doing projects for external customers, changes in top management are associated with improvements in work climate and the cost of the PMO. In these organizations, the conflict inherent in customer/supplier relations is much less salient.

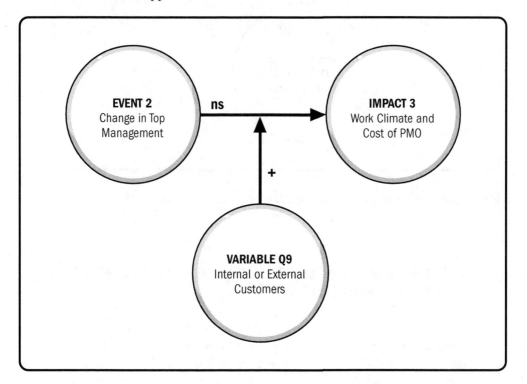

Figure 8.16. Pure Moderator Effect of Having External Project Customers

There is no significant association between the importance of issues related to collaboration and accountability (Issue 2) and Impact 3. However, in organizations that report that the PMO transition was put in place with little difficulty a positive association was found between Issue 2 and Impact 3. One would expect that changes put in place to improve collaboration and accountability would produce improvements in the working climate. However, if the implementation met with problems of resistance to change or other human relations issues, one would not expect to find this association. The moderating effect of the ease of implementation can be interpreted as supporting this explanation.

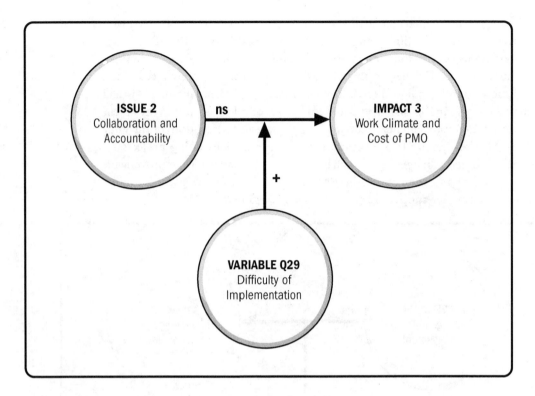

Figure 8.17. Pure Moderator Effect of the Difficulty of Implementation.

8.3 Discussion of the Findings Related to Mediating and Moderating Effects

From the outset, one of the most important objectives of this research has been to identify patterns in which changes to PMOs are related to both the drivers of the changes and their impact on the organization. In other words, the goal has been to find which drivers lead to which changes to PMOs, which in turn lead to improvements in the organization. The correlation analysis presented in Chapter Seven did not identify any such patterns. The aim of the analysis of mediator and moderator effects was to identify more subtle patterns. A few such patterns were identified, although it should be noted that the mediator and moderator effects explain less of the variance than the direct effects.

When a particular issue is the driver of the change and the impact is on this same issue, the pattern is easier to interpret. When another issue is the driver of the change, the interpretation is much more speculative. The discussion highlights changes where the impact was on the issue driving the change or when events were the drivers of change. The quasi-moderator effects are much more difficult to interpret and have not been considered in the discussion.

8.3.1 Patterns Related to Improvements in Portfolio Management and Methods (Impact 1)

One such pattern was identified in improvements in portfolio management and methods. The moderating effect of decreases in the scope of control and the controlling nature of the PMO's role (Change 2) on the relationship between the importance of portfolio management issues and improvements in these issues, shown in Figure 8.8, is the simplest and most direct of these patterns. When portfolio management and methods are an issue, organizations implement changes to the PMO to improve these issues. If decreasing the scope of control of the PMO is among the changes, the improvements tend to be greater.

8.3.2 Patterns Related to Improvements in Collaboration, Accountability and Skill (Impact 2)

The importance of issues related to collaboration and accountability and the importance of external events as drivers of change both have important direct effects on improvements to these issues. In addition to these direct effects, a complex network with two mediator and two moderator effects was also identified. The direct effect of the importance of these issues on improvements is mediated by PMO's autonomy, as shown in Figure 8.5. In addition, the direct effect of external events on improvements to these issues is mediated by the importance of these issues. In other words, the importance of external events increases both the importance of collaboration and accountability as an organizational issue and improvements in these issues, as shown by the partial mediator effect of these issues in the relationship between external events and improvements in these issues in Figure 8.3.

The level of project management maturity is a moderator of both direct effects, but its moderator effect is somewhat contradictory; it moderates the direct effect of the importance of these issues positively and the direct effect of external events negatively, as shown in Figure 8.11. But external events increase the importance of these issues, which in turn increases the level of improvement. Thus, when external events are important drivers of change, the positive and negative moderating effects of project management maturity at least partially cancel each other out. Since the moderating effects are not very strong, the combined effect of positive and negative moderation is most likely to be negligible. Thus, the positive moderating effect of project management maturity is only present when external events are not important drivers of PMO change.

8.3.3 Patterns Related to Improvements in Work Climate and Cost of PMO

Only one pattern linking drivers to changes in the PMO to impacts was identified. The moderating effect of increases in the functions of the PMO and its supportiveness (CHANGE 1) was shown to have an effect on the relationship between external events as drivers of change and improvements in work climate and the cost of the PMO, as shown in Figure 8.15. However, this relation only holds when external events are very important as drivers of change.

8.3.4   The Logic of PMO Transformations is Primarily Context-Specific

The search for general patterns in the transformations of PMOs has yielded some partial results, as shown in the sections above. The moderator effects on improvements in portfolio management and methods and work climate and the cost of the PMO are straightforward and easy to interpret and to translate into guidelines for management action. The mediator and moderator effects on improvements in collaboration, accountability and skills are much more complex and do not translate as readily into simple prescriptions for management practice. Furthermore, the mediator and moderator effects only explain a very small portion of the total variance. Much of the transformation process remains unexplained. The authors have concluded that many of the transformation processes are context-specific.

8.3.5 Moderating Effects of Project Management Maturity

Project management maturity was shown to have a pure moderating effect on the relation between three different drivers of PMO change and improvements in collaboration, accountability and skill (IMPACT 2). The fact that the moderating effect is a pure effect means that the level of maturity had no significant direct effect on IMPACT 2. However, the situations in which issues related to collaboration and accountability are important are the situations where improvements in these issues are the most important. In these situations, the level of maturity has two positive moderating effects and one negative moderating effect. This finding provides a possible insight into the nature of project management maturity, which is generally conceived based on the same logic as ISO and CMMI process models. The primary element of all these models is the definition and management of processes, project management processes in this case. However, these models also include elements of monitoring performance of processes and of continuous improvement processes. These elements are more closely linked to the management of organizational change. The moderator effects of the level of project management maturity may be an indication of the role higher levels of project management maturity play in process change and improvement in general and in PMO transformations in particular.

The level of maturity is not related to the specific changes that are made to PMOs. In some situations, mature organizations seem to make better choices or to implement them more smoothly, but the choices are related to the context.

This is a sort of second-order capability, not the capability to put in place certain practices or structures but an ability to make informed choices as to what changes to make and how to implement them. This is an aspect of project management maturity that has not been developed in the literature.

8.3.6 Organizational Change

A change in a PMO is an organizational change, the implementation of which can be easy or difficult, fast or slow; it can either be accompanied by change management practices or not. All three of these aspects of organizational change were shown to have mediating or moderating effects related to the improvements in organizations. As shown in section 6.2.3, about half of the transformations of PMOs were not accompanied by change management practices. These findings support the use of change management practices when modifying a PMO.

8.4 Key Findings Related to Mediating and Moderating Effects

1. The analysis of mediating and moderating effects did not reveal important general patterns among the variables in the form of particular drivers of change leading to specific changes in PMO and in turn to specific improvements. However, some significant findings did shed light on specific situations.
2. The pattern that leads the most directly to guidelines for managerial practice is: When portfolio management and methods are important issues, decreases in the scope and controlling nature of the PMO's mandate are associated with greater improvements in these issues.
3. Making significant changes to a PMO is an organizational change and should be managed as such.
4. Project management maturity does not have a direct effect on organizational improvements. It does have moderator effects in some situations. This may reflect the effect of the monitoring, management, and continuous improvement functions found at higher levels of maturity.

CHAPTER NINE: DISCUSSION

This section of the monograph is intended to bring together and to discuss the most significant results from this research. It is difficult work because of the richness of the data. Up until this point, results have been presented in a sequential approach, more or less as the research unfolded. Key findings have been presented at the end of Chapters Five through Eight. These present the most important results from the succession of analyses that constituted the empirical work in this research project: the qualitative case studies and the statistical analysis of principal components, correlations, mediator effects and moderator effects. The objective of the present chapter is to highlight and discuss the most significant results.

9.1 Modeling the Transformation of PMOs

As explained in Chapter Three, we adopted a multi-phase and multi-method methodology, working within a strong complementary framework. Referring to the Van de Ven and Poole (2005) typology of approaches for studying organizational change, our research considered the PMO as a *thing* rather than as a verb or a process of organizing. These authors identified two approaches within this view: process method and variance method. This research made use of both methods in a complementary way. The 17 case studies in the first qualitative phase described the process of transforming each PMO from one state to the next through the telling of each of these PMO histories and the sequence of events and issues that led to the change and its impacts. The objective of the first phase was to capture rich detail and to make certain that the research was grounded in reality. A relatively large sample of case studies was used in order to produce results that are more representative of the general phenomenon.

The second, survey-based quantitative phase continued with the process view of the PMO transformation, but through a variance method. The same process model was used as the basis for the construction of the survey instrument; variables were defined based on a summary of the 17 case studies. The instrument was developed and tested with the 17 qualitative case study organizations.

Previous research has shown that PMOs change frequently (Hobbs & Aubry, 2010). The objective of the present research is to better understand the transformations of PMOs. Based on previous work by Aubry (2007), the conceptual model of the PMO transformation process shown in Figure 2.2 was developed and refined. This model is based on a process view of the organizational change.

During the qualitative case studies, the model proved to be a good representation of the transformation process. Managers interviewed were able to tell the story of the transformation of their PMO and relate it to the conceptual model. The case studies confirmed the premise that periods of relative stability are punctuated by periods of relatively rapid change and that these changes are significant.

During the qualitative case studies, the model provided a framework for capturing and making sense of the historical transformation process and the contextually-specific details of each case. Based on both the qualitative and quantitative data, an understanding was developed of the dynamics of each case. The story of how and why each PMO changed was based on the organization's history and a complex and dynamic situation that involved multiple players, events, and issues, which unfolded over time.

The results of the qualitative case studies informed the survey that followed. The objectives of the quantitative study were to:

- Discover how representative the observations made during the case studies were
- Identify patterns in the transformation process.

The survey was much more successful in accomplishing the first objective than the second. The following sections present and discuss the main findings.

9.2 Why Do PMOs Change?

The results from the 17 case studies identified 32 drivers of PMO change: five events external to the organization, nine events internal to the organization and eighteen issues that led to changes to the PMO. The survey results showed that all of these drivers are important in explaining PMO change in the more general context of the survey. The differences in the importance of the drivers were relatively small, meaning that PMO change can be driven by a wide variety of events and issues. The survey also showed that the drivers identified in the 17 cases were present in many other PMO transformations and were not just idiosyncratic details of a particular case.

The principal component analysis identified underlying patterns among the drivers of PMO change. The analysis grouped the majority of the drivers into six conceptually consistent factors. Thus, the principal component analysis captured some of the interactions among the drivers of change, but only those that were present in large numbers of PMO transformations.

The case study research showed that in each case a complex interplay of several events and issues drove PMO change and that the process leading up to the change unfolded over time. The analysis could not capture the details of the drivers of change in each case, nor the complex interaction among different drivers within their historical context.

9.3 The Implementation of the Change to the PMO

The survey confirmed that the changes to the PMOs were significant and often difficult to implement. The survey also showed that changes to the PMOs are generally implemented rather quickly; more than 75% of the changes studied occurred in less than 12 months. The change to a PMO is an organizational change and the results show that these changes are considered significant. Somewhat surprisingly, approximately 50% of respondents reported that the PMO change was not accompanied by an organizational change management process. The research was not designed specifically to measure the effects of the use of change management practices. However, the analysis did reveal that the use of change management has several significant mediating and moderating effects within the transformation process, which is an indication that the use of change management has an effect and that organizations should consider PMO change as an important organizational change and make use of these practices.

9.4 The Changes to the PMOs

The research investigated the nature of the changes to the PMOs by comparing the descriptions of a large number of PMO characteristics before and after the changes. Principal component analysis was used to group the majority of the changes into three reliable factors, thus revealing an underlying pattern among the many changes to PMOs. Here again, principal component analysis identifies patterns that are repeated in large numbers of PMO transformations and as such provides the basis for a more general understanding of the nature of these changes.

9.5 The Failure to Identify Patterns in the Transformation Process

It was possible in the 17 case studies to understand how the context had unfolded and how the drivers had led to the changes that were made to the PMO. Several analyses were performed in search of patterns linking drivers of change to changes in the PMOs. The analyses were performed using the factors identified through principal component analysis, in part because the sample size was too small to identify such patterns among the many individual drivers and changes to PMOs. The first approach was to test for correlations between drivers of change and changes made to PMOs. No significant patterns were identified. Further analysis of mediator and moderator effects did reveal some partial patterns and some complex interactions. These were not enough to identify general patterns, but were illustrative of the complex interactions occurring during the transformation process.

The failure to identify general patterns in the transformation process leads the authors to ask why these general patterns were not apparent. Several explanations may be considered:

- The reduction of drivers and changes to PMOs to a small number of factors simplifies the description of the transformation process. This description may not be rich enough to capture the transformation process. If the sample size had been much larger, more sophisticated analyses might have identified more patterns in the transformation process without relying on principal component analysis to reduce the data.

- Both the qualitative and quantitative results showed that multiple drivers are involved in each PMO transformation. Given the number of possible drivers, the number of possible combinations involved in any single case is very large. It may be that despite the pattern underlying the principal component analysis, each case is more or less unique. The drivers in the quantitative study have been treated asynchronously, while in reality the process that leads to a PMO transformation unfolds over time. Thus the sequence in which drivers manifest themselves in each case may be different. In addition to the consideration of the drivers identified in the study, it is likely that other factors help explain the decision to transform a PMO. All together, the inventory of the drivers is a rather limited representation of the dynamics behind a decision to transform a PMO.

- The PMO transformation is a process of organizational change that unfolds over time. The conceptual framework is a process model but it reduces the historical perspective to four elements:
  - The inventory of the drivers of change
  - The description of the PMO before the change
  - The description of the PMO after the change
  - The impact of the change on the issues that drove the change.

This is a simplification of the social and historical process that leads to a change in a PMO. Each of the elements as measured in the survey is a simplification, and reducing the process to these four elements is also a simplification.

- The conceptual model assumes a linear process in a single direction and does not allow for feedback loops. It is possible that only systems models with complex interaction effects including feedback loops could capture the underlying patterns.

- The conceptual model implicitly applies the rational lens or perspective adopted from Rajagopalan and Spreitzer (1996). The process may be as political as it is rational.

- Many of these limitations are related to the use of the variance method. This method is difficult when applied to phenomenon where there is "influence from different factors, including critical events, multiple causes operating unevenly in different parts of the organization and at different points in time, causes operating across greatly different time scales, and sequences of events that chain together to lead up to some outcome" (Van de Ven & Poole, 2005, p. 1388). In PMO transformations, these results show that there are multiple factors at play, some of which might be dramatic or accessory, at an internal micro-level or external macro-level, etc. This limitation could explain why external events do not show up as important drivers but provoke far-reaching organizational change when they occur.

CHAPTER TEN: CONCLUSION

This research focused on understanding the phenomenon of PMOs in transition. The major result from this research outlines a paradigm shift regarding changes to PMOs. It provides some empirical evidence that the transition of a PMO from one configuration to the next is not a question of being right or wrong. PMO transformations can be understood rather as a multi-level dynamic process anchored in a specific organizational context.

The analysis presented here makes several contributions to the study of organizations in general and to the study of PMOs in particular. It confirms that the PMO is deeply embedded in its host organization, and that the two actively take part in the transforming process. This result is in line with the research on the value of project management where a "fit" should exist with the organizational context (Thomas & Mullaly, 2008). The study also shows that internal events and tensions are among the primary drivers of the reconfiguration of PMOs. The playing out of these drivers brings into focus the importance of organizational politics. The analysis shows that PMOs and, more generally, the structures put in place to manage multiple projects are part of a political system that plays an important role in organizations (Morgan, 1989; Winter & Szczepanek, 2009). In the project management literature, power and politics are often treated with an instrumental approach through risk management and stakeholder management (Magenau & Pinto, 2004). The analysis here shows that power and politics should be examined at the organizational level and integrated into organizational project management.

The authors believe that this research has partially filled the void of empirical evidence regarding PMO transitions. More research on PMOs, and globally on organizational project management, is recommended. Future contributions from the project management research community should aim to better anchor the research theoretically within organizational theory or other solid theoretical foundations.

Two limitations have been identified within this research. The first is the focus on a unique transformation as opposed to a continuous evolutionary process. This focus was essential to understand the process, but it should be understood as a partial view of the reality, where outcomes from the transformations contain within them what will become the conditions and drivers for the next PMO transformation. The second limitation relates to the partial support of results from the early phases qualitative case studies of this research by the quantitative results from the survey. One explanation for the lack of results may be related to the use of a questionnaire to explore a process. Research on process should rather be based upon qualitative approaches answering *why* and *how* questions. Questionnaires relate to a variable approach, answering *what* questions (Van de Ven, 2007). From the beginning, it was known that the goal of this research is determined by a process. This led to a qualitative study as a start, but results from qualitative research lack the capacity for generalization. Therefore, there is a need to validate the results of qualitative research through questionnaires. This methodology was adopted here, but only produced partial results.

APPENDICES

Appendix A PMO Descriptive Model

	Classes of data	Element of data
PMO context	**Organizational context**	• Economic sector • Public or private • Size of organization • Percentage of resources that Report to the same management as the PMO Manager or that are matrixed throughout the organization • Internal or external project clients • Single or multiple project customers • Level of organizational project management maturity • Supportiveness of organizational culture
	Type of projects in the PMO mandate	• Scope expressed as the number of people working on the project • Scope in terms of duration • The type of product or service delivered* • The primary performance criteria of the PMO's projects* • The inclusion of post-delivery activities within project scope* • Involvement in outsourcing contracts*

PMO description	**Structural characteristics**	• The name used to identify the PMO
		• Time to implement the PMO
		• Location within the organizational hierarchy
		• Relationship(s) with other PMO(s) in the same organization
		• Staff of PMO (other than project/program managers)
		• Size expressed as the number of people working on the project. This is also a measure of the size of the PMO
		    ▪ Experience of the staff*
		    ▪ Professional background of the staff*
		    ▪ Presence of business analysts or business architects among the staff*
		• Age of the PMO
		• Percentage of projects within the mandate of the PMO
		• Percentage of project managers within the PMO
		• Decision-making authority of the PMO
		• The status of the project management methodology
		    • Homegrown or brought in from outside*
		    • Use is compulsory or discretionary*
		    • Degree to which methods are actually followed*
		• The adequacy of funding of the PMO*
		• The means of funding including the billing for services*

	Roles or functions	1. Monitor and control project performance 2. Develop and implement standards and competencies 3. Multi-project management 4. Strategic management 5. Organizational learning 6. Management of customer interfaces 7. Recruit, select, evaluate and determine salaries for project managers 8. Execute specialized tasks for project managers
Performance	**Perceived performance**	• Legitimacy, reported in response to the question, "Has the relevance or even the existence of the PMO been seriously questioned in recent years?" • Contribution to project/program performance.

Appendix B Questionnaire

PMOs IN TRANSITION

General Information on the Organisation

In compliance with the policies of the Research Committee of the University of Quebec in Montreal (UQAM), all the information provided will remain strictly confidential.

1. The organisation is of which type?

○ Private enterprise

○ Public sector organisation

○ Non Governmental Organisation (NGO) or a not-for-profit organisation

2. The primary activities of the organisation are in which economic sector?

[▼]

3. Primarily, the projects within the mandate of the PMO produce what type of deliverable?

○ Engineering or construction

○ New product or service development

○ Consulting services

○ Information system or information technology

○ Business processes

Other (please specify)

[   ]

4. What is your present position?

○ Project manager   ○ Senior Executive

○ Programme manager   ○ Manager elsewhere in the organisation

○ Portfolio manager   ○ Professional in the PMO

○ PMO manager   ○ Professional elsewhere in the organisation

○ Other manager in the PMO   ○ Consultant

Other (please specify)

[   ]

5. What is the total number of employees?
(For large organisations including multi-nationals, please indicate the total number of employees.)

○ 1 to 100   ○ 501 to 1000   ○ 10,001 to 30,000

○ 101 to 500   ○ 1001 to 10,000   ○ More than 30,000

PMOs IN TRANSITION

6. Which of the follow categories best describes the level of project management maturity of the organisation?

○ Initial Level - ad hoc and chaotic; relies on the competence of individuals not the organisation's.

○ Repeatable Level - there is a project management system and plans are based on previous experience.

○ Defined Level - common, organisation wide understanding of project management activities, roles and responsibilities.

○ Managed Level - stable and measured processes against organisational goals; variations are identified and addressed.

○ Optimising Level - the entire organisation is focused on continuous improvement

7. In which country does the PMO operate primarily?

[▼]

If the PMO operates in multiple countries, please indicate the other countries:

[   ]

8. Primarily, the projects in which the PMO is involved are for:

○ One customer

○ Several customers

9. Primarily, the projects in which the PMO is involved are delivered to:

○ Internal units within your organisation

○ External organisations

10. On the average, how many people are actively involved in a typical project in the PMO?

○ Less than 10   ○ 76 to 100

○ 11 to 25   ○ 101 to 200

○ 26 to 50   ○ more than 200

○ 51 to 75

A Major Change to the PMO: Reasons for the Change and its Impacts

The following section of the survey examines the recent change to the PMO you are describing. It focuses on reasons for the change and its impacts.

11. How long ago was the change initiated:

○ Less than 1 year   ○ 1 to 2 years   ○ 2 to 3 years   ○ 3 to 4 years   ○ 4 to 5 years   ○ More than 5 years

12. The amplitude of the change was?

○ 1   ○ 2   ○ 3   ○ 4   ○ 5   ○ 6   ○ 7   ○ 8   ○ 9
Minor   Radical

PMOs IN TRANSITION

13. Was a previous PMO shutdown prior to the implementation of the new PMO?

◯ No

◯ Yes

14. Indicate the importance of the following external factors as drivers of the change in the PMO (the middle position 5 is omitted):

	1 No importance	2	3	4	6	7	8	9 High importance
Change in global or local economy	◯	◯	◯	◯	◯	◯	◯	◯
Change in your industry or market	◯	◯	◯	◯	◯	◯	◯	◯
Change in the national or local political environment	◯	◯	◯	◯	◯	◯	◯	◯
Change in the regulatory environment	◯	◯	◯	◯	◯	◯	◯	◯
Pressures related to social responsibilities, ethics or environmental impact	◯	◯	◯	◯	◯	◯	◯	◯

Other (please specify)

15. Indicate the importance of the following internal factors as drivers of the change in the PMO (the middle position 5 is omitted):

	1 No importance	2	3	4	6	7	8	9 High importance
New ownership through merger or acquisition	◯	◯	◯	◯	◯	◯	◯	◯
New CEO	◯	◯	◯	◯	◯	◯	◯	◯
Changes in the composition of the executive team other than the CEO	◯	◯	◯	◯	◯	◯	◯	◯
New PMO manager	◯	◯	◯	◯	◯	◯	◯	◯
New vision and/or strategy of the executive team	◯	◯	◯	◯	◯	◯	◯	◯
Broad organisational restructuring	◯	◯	◯	◯	◯	◯	◯	◯
Unsatisfactory project performance or failures	◯	◯	◯	◯	◯	◯	◯	◯
Competition with other parts of the organisation either for mandates or for resources	◯	◯	◯	◯	◯	◯	◯	◯
Changes in the total project workload i.e. number, size or complexity of projects	◯	◯	◯	◯	◯	◯	◯	◯

Other (please specify)

16. Related to the change in total project workload, the change was:

◯ 1   ◯ 2   ◯ 3   ◯ 4   ◯ 5   ◯ 6   ◯ 7   ◯ 8   ◯ 9
Major decrease   No change   Major increase

There will be two questions on each of the following issues:
Before the change: to what extent was each of the following issues an important reason for making the change?
After the change: to what extent did the change have an impact on each of these issues?

PMOs IN TRANSITION

17. Issues related to organisational context:

REASONS OF CHANGE

1: No importance (the middle position 5 is omitted)
9: High importance

	1	2	3	4	6	7	8	9
Organisational commitment to project management	○	○	○	○	○	○	○	○
Customer and stakeholder relations	○	○	○	○	○	○	○	○
Project management and line collaboration	○	○	○	○	○	○	○	○
Tensions or conflicts within the organisation	○	○	○	○	○	○	○	○
Accountability for projects	○	○	○	○	○	○	○	○
Synergy among project managers	○	○	○	○	○	○	○	○

18. Issues related to organisational context:

IMPACTS AFTER THE CHANGE

1: Deterioration 5: No change 9: Improvement

	1	2	3	4	5	6	7	8	9
Organisational commitment to project management	○	○	○	○	○	○	○	○	○
Customer and stakeholder relations	○	○	○	○	○	○	○	○	○
Project management and line collaboration	○	○	○	○	○	○	○	○	○
Tensions or conflicts within the organisation	○	○	○	○	○	○	○	○	○
Accountability for projects	○	○	○	○	○	○	○	○	○
Synergy among project managers	○	○	○	○	○	○	○	○	○

PMOs IN TRANSITION

19. Issues related to the human resources:

REASONS OF CHANGE

1: No importance (the middle position 5 is omitted)
9: High importance

	1	2	3	4	6	7	8	9
Project management skill level	○	○	○	○	○	○	○	○
Work climate	○	○	○	○	○	○	○	○
Work-family equilibrium	○	○	○	○	○	○	○	○

20. Issues related to the human resources:

IMPACTS AFTER THE CHANGE

1: Deterioration 5: No change 9: Improvement

	1	2	3	4	5	6	7	8	9
Project management skill level	○	○	○	○	○	○	○	○	○
Work climate	○	○	○	○	○	○	○	○	○
Work-family equilibrium	○	○	○	○	○	○	○	○	○

21. Issues related to performance:

REASONS OF CHANGE

1: No importance (the middle position 5 is omitted)
9: High importance

	1	2	3	4	6	7	8	9
Cost of PMO	○	○	○	○	○	○	○	○
Project performance	○	○	○	○	○	○	○	○
Business performance	○	○	○	○	○	○	○	○

PMOs IN TRANSITION

22. Issues related to performance:

IMPACTS AFTER THE CHANGE

1: Deterioration 5: No change 9: Improvement

	1	2	3	4	5	6	7	8	9
Cost of PMO	○	○	○	○	○	○	○	○	○
Project performance	○	○	○	○	○	○	○	○	○
Business performance	○	○	○	○	○	○	○	○	○

23. Issues related to project management processes:

REASONS OF CHANGE

1: No importance (the middle position 5 is omitted)
9: High importance

	1	2	3	4	6	7	8	9
Project management maturity	○	○	○	○	○	○	○	○
Project alignment with strategy	○	○	○	○	○	○	○	○
Availability of relevant information to decision makers	○	○	○	○	○	○	○	○
Project selection	○	○	○	○	○	○	○	○
Allocation of resources across multiple projects	○	○	○	○	○	○	○	○
Fit between project management methods and project characteristics	○	○	○	○	○	○	○	○
Standardisation of project management methods	○	○	○	○	○	○	○	○

PMOs IN TRANSITION

24. Issues related to project management processes:

IMPACTS AFTER THE CHANGE

1: Deterioration 5: No change 9: Improvement

```
          1  2  3  4  5  6  7  8  9
```

Project management maturity ○○○○○○○○○

Project alignment with strategy ○○○○○○○○○

Availability of relevant information to decision makers ○○○○○○○○○

Project selection ○○○○○○○○○

Allocation of resources across multiple projects ○○○○○○○○○

Fit between project management methods and project characteristics ○○○○○○○○○

Standardisation of project management methods ○○○○○○○○○

25. Related to the standardisation of project management processes, the issue was?

○ 1 Not enough standardisation ○ 2 ○ 3 ○ 4 ○ 5 Adequate standardisation ○ 6 ○ 7 ○ 8 ○ 9 Too much standardisation

26. Were other issues important reasons for changes to the PMO?

27. Did the change in the PMO have other important impacts?

28. Was the change in the PMO accompanied by organisational change management processes?

○ No

○ Yes

○ Don't know

PMOs IN TRANSITION

29. The implementation was:

○ 1 Very easy, no problems of importance ○ 2 ○ 3 ○ 4 ○ 5 ○ 6 ○ 7 ○ 8 ○ 9 Very difficult, major problems ○ Don't know

30. How long did it take to implement this PMO change?

○ Instantaneously
○ Less than 3 months
○ 3-6 months
○ 6-9 months

○ 9-12 months
○ More than a year
○ Implementation was abandoned
○ Can't answer, implementation is not completed

A Major Change to the PMO: Roles or Functions

The following section of the survey examines the recent change to the PMO you are describing. It focuses on the roles or functions this PMO fulfils at two different times: before the change and after.

31. PMOs fill many roles or functions. Indicate the importance of the following functions within the PMO's mandate:

BEFORE THE CHANGE

1: No importance
9: High importance

	1	2	3	4	5	6	7	8	9
Monitor and control project performance, including the development of Projects Information System and the reporting function	○	○	○	○	○	○	○	○	○
Develop and implement standard methodologies, processes and tools	○	○	○	○	○	○	○	○	○
Develop the competency of project personnel including training and mentoring	○	○	○	○	○	○	○	○	○
Multi-project management including programme and portfolio management, coordination and allocation of resources between projects	○	○	○	○	○	○	○	○	○
Strategic management including participation in strategic planning and benefits management	○	○	○	○	○	○	○	○	○
Organisational learning including the management of lessons learned, audits and monitoring of PMO performance	○	○	○	○	○	○	○	○	○
Management of customer interfaces	○	○	○	○	○	○	○	○	○
Recruit, select, evaluate and determine salaries for Project Managers	○	○	○	○	○	○	○	○	○
Execute specialized tasks for Project Managers, e.g. preparation of schedules	○	○	○	○	○	○	○	○	○

Page 8

PMOs IN TRANSITION

32. PMOs fill many roles or functions. Indicate the importance of the following functions within the PMO's mandate:

AFTER THE CHANGE

1: No importance
9: High importance

	1	2	3	4	5	6	7	8	9
Monitor and control project performance, including the development of Projects Information System and the reporting function	○	○	○	○	○	○	○	○	○
Develop and implement standard methodologies, processes and tools	○	○	○	○	○	○	○	○	○
Develop the competency of project personnel including training and mentoring	○	○	○	○	○	○	○	○	○
Multi-project management including programme and portfolio management, coordination and allocation of resources between projects	○	○	○	○	○	○	○	○	○
Strategic management including participation in strategic planning and benefits management	○	○	○	○	○	○	○	○	○
Organisational learning including the management of lessons learned, audits and monitoring of PMO performance	○	○	○	○	○	○	○	○	○
Management of customer interfaces	○	○	○	○	○	○	○	○	○
Recruit, select, evaluate and determine salaries for Project Managers	○	○	○	○	○	○	○	○	○
Execute specialized tasks for Project Managers, e.g. preparation of schedules	○	○	○	○	○	○	○	○	○

33. The PMO can be supportive and/or controlling. To what extent was the PMO:

BEFORE THE CHANGE

	1 Not at all	2	3	4	5	6	7	8	9 Very
Supportive	○	○	○	○	○	○	○	○	○
Controlling	○	○	○	○	○	○	○	○	○

34. The PMO can be supportive and/or controlling. To what extent is the PMO:

AFTER THE CHANGE

	1 Not at all	2	3	4	5	6	7	8	9 Very
Supportive	○	○	○	○	○	○	○	○	○
Controlling	○	○	○	○	○	○	○	○	○

A Major Change to the PMO: Structural Characteristics

The following section of the survey examines the recent change to the PMO you are describing. It focuses on the structural characteristics of this PMO at two different times: before the change and after.

PMOs IN TRANSITION

35. PMO's location within the organisation?

BEFORE THE CHANGE

- ○ IT
- ○ Finance
- ○ Human Resources
- ○ Other functional unit
- ○ Operations
- ○ Business unit
- ○ Outside these units and reporting directly to a senior executive
- ○ Other (please specify)

  [   ]

36. PMO's location within the organisation?

AFTER THE CHANGE

- ○ IT
- ○ Finance
- ○ Human Resources
- ○ Other functional unit
- ○ Operations
- ○ Business unit
- ○ Outside these units and reporting directly to a senior executive

Other (please specify)

[   ]

37. Interdependence with other PMOs?

	YES	NO
Before the change	○	○
After the change	○	○

Page 10

150

PMOs IN TRANSITION

38. Did the change to the PMO involve:

◯ A merger of 2 or more PMOs?

◯ A division of one PMO to 2 or more PMOs?

If needed, please describe the change in your own words

[   ]

39. The PMO's access to the top management (the middle position 5 is omitted)?

BEFORE THE CHANGE

◯ 1   ◯ 2   ◯ 3   ◯ 4   ◯ 6   ◯ 7   ◯ 8   ◯ 9

Very easy   Very difficult

40. The PMO's access to the top management (the middle position 5 is omitted)?

AFTER THE CHANGE

◯ 1   ◯ 2   ◯ 3   ◯ 4   ◯ 6   ◯ 7   ◯ 8   ◯ 9

Very easy   Very difficult

For the following questions please respond in relation to the organisational entity in which the PMO is active. This may be the entire organisation, a division, a department or any other part of the organisation.

41. The number of projects executed simultaneously within the unit?

BEFORE THE CHANGE [   ]
AFTER THE CHANGE [   ]

42. Percentage of these projects within PMO's mandate?

BEFORE THE CHANGE: % [   ]
AFTER THE CHANGE: % [   ]

43. Percentage of project managers reporting to the PMO manager?

BEFORE THE CHANGE: % [   ]
AFTER THE CHANGE: % [   ]

44. Excluding Project Managers if any, number of people, expressed in full time equivalents, working in the PMO? (Including the person responsible for the PMO).

BEFORE THE CHANGE [   ]
AFTER THE CHANGE [   ]

PMOs IN TRANSITION

45. The hierarchical level to which the PMO reports is:

○ 1　○ 2　○ 3　○ 4　○ 5　○ 6　○ 7　○ 8　○ 9
Much
lower
　　　　　　　　　　　No
　　　　　　　　　　　change
　　　　　　　　　　　　　　　　　　　　　　　Much
　　　　　　　　　　　　　　　　　　　　　　　higher

46. Level of the PMO's decision-making authority?

BEFORE THE CHANGE

1: No authority at all
9: Very significant authority

○ 1　○ 2　○ 3　○ 4　○ 5　○ 6　○ 7　○ 8　○ 9

47. Level of the PMO's decision-making authority?

AFTER THE CHANGE

1: No authority at all
9: Very significant authority

○ 1　○ 2　○ 3　○ 4　○ 5　○ 6　○ 7　○ 8　○ 9

48. The manager to whom the person responsible for the PMO reports had authority over what percentage of the human resources that work on the PMO's projects?

BEFORE THE CHANGE: % [＿＿＿＿＿＿＿＿＿＿＿＿＿＿]
AFTER THE CHANGE: % [＿＿＿＿＿＿＿＿＿＿＿＿＿＿]

49. Funding for the PMO?

BEFORE THE CHANGE

1: Clearly insufficient 5: Adequate
9: Overly generous

○ 1　○ 2　○ 3　○ 4　○ 5　○ 6　○ 7　○ 8　○ 9

PMOs IN TRANSITION

50. Funding for the PMO?

AFTER THE CHANGE

1: Clearly insufficient 5: Adequate
9: Overly generous

◯ 1 ◯ 2 ◯ 3 ◯ 4 ◯ 5 ◯ 6 ◯ 7 ◯ 8 ◯ 9

51. To what extent did the organisational culture support the PMO (the middle position 5 is omitted)?

BEFORE THE CHANGE

◯ 1 ◯ 2 ◯ 3 ◯ 4 ◯ 6 ◯ 7 ◯ 8 ◯ 9 Very
No   significant
support   support

52. To what extent does the organisational culture support the PMO (the middle position 5 is omitted)?

AFTER THE CHANGE

◯ 1 ◯ 2 ◯ 3 ◯ 4 ◯ 6 ◯ 7 ◯ 8 ◯ 9 Very
No   significant
support   support

53. PMO's accountability for project performance?

BEFORE THE CHANGE

1: No accountability (the middle position 5 is omitted)
9: Totally accountable

         1 2 3 4 6 7 8 9
Scope,   ◯◯◯◯◯◯◯◯
costs &
schedule
Benefits ◯◯◯◯◯◯◯◯

PMOs IN TRANSITION

54. PMO'S ACCOUNTABILITY FOR PROJECT PERFORMANCE?

AFTER THE CHANGE

1: No accountability (the middle position 5 is omitted)
9: Totally accountable

Scope, costs & schedule — 1 2 3 4 6 7 8 9 ○○○○○○○○

Benefits ○○○○○○○

55. If you wish to receive a copy of the results of this survey, please provide your e-mail address:

Email Address: [ ]

Description of changes to the another PMO
If you are able to describe changes to another PMO, we invite you to record your data by selecting "Finish button" and restarting the survey from the site www.pmo-survey.esg.uqam.ca/

Sending the survey to another person
If you know someone who could describe a change to a different PMO, please invite him or her to do so and provide the address www.pmo-survey.esg.uqam.ca/

The survey results accumulate automatically. You can access the results by clicking on "Finish button" below. You can save the address of the results page in order to access the results at a later date.

Thank you for your collaboration.

Research team
Project: PMOs in Transition
Project Management Research Chair at UQAM

Appendix C Typology and Definition of Drivers

Group of Drivers	Driver	Definition
1. **External events**	Economic	Above average changes in production, exchange, distribution, and consumption of goods or services on a national or international basis.
	Industrial/Market	Changes in or emergence of factors in a company's industry, such as automobile or banking.
	Political	Change in government policies or appearance of international laws or standards, such as Basel II or Sarbanes-Oxley.
	Social responsibilities	Ethical or ideological factors external to the corporation.
	Customer	Factors stemming from a company's customers or clients.
2. **Internal events**	Growth in projects	A significant increase in the number or size of projects within an organization.
	New owner or merger	A change in corporate ownership, such as a take-over or merger.
	New strategy	A recent change in strategy (both corporate or business unit level)
	Reorganization	A recent reorganization affecting the PMO
	New CEO	A recent change in the Chief Executive Officer (CEO) or head of the corporation
	New member of Executive Board	A change or joining of a new member of the board of directors of the corporation
	New PMO Manager	Changes or appointment of a new PMO manager
	Project failure	Change or constantly high failure rate in projects
	Complexity in projects	Change in complexity levels of projects
	Internal competition	Factors related to inter-organizational rivalry, competition or other forms of out-performing other parts of the organization
3. **Organizational context issues**	Political issues	Factors of organizational political nature
	Organizational commitment for project management	Factors of organizational commitment for project management as a discipline
	Client and stakeholder relations	Factors related to the relationship with customers, clients or other stakeholders of the firm
	Project management collaboration with line organization	Factors related to the way line and matrix management work together and interacts
	Accountability for projects	Factors related to new accountabilities for projects and their results
	Synergy among project managers	Factors related to changes in or intentions to achieve synergies among and across PMOs
4. **Project management process issues**	Innovativeness	Factors related to changes in the way innovation is used in the firm, or innovative ways of doing business are pursued
	PMO costs	Factors related to changes in real costs or evaluation thereof

	Agility	Factors related to the use of Agile/Scrum or other new methodologies
	Standardized project management process	Factors related to the application of standardized processes and compliance with it
	Control of project portfolio	Factors related to the change in control of the project portfolio
	Skill allocation	Factors related to the change in assigning skills to projects
	Maturity in project management	Factors related to the organizational maturity in project management
	Project alignment with strategy	Factors related to the alignment of projects with the organization's strategy
Human relations issues	HR perspective	Factors related to human resources and their management
	PM skills development	Factors related to the development of project management skills within the organization.
Performance issues	Project performance	Factors related to project deliveries and results
	Business performance	Factors related to the business performance of the organization

Appendix D Alignment Between Constructs and Questions

Construct	External drivers for change	Internal drivers for change	PMO transformation
Items	Q14 External events	Q15 Internal events	Q11 Time since PMO change
		Q16 Project workload: decrease or increase	Q12 Amplitude of the change
		Q17 Issues related to organizational context	Q13 PMO shutdown before
		Q19 Issues related to human relations	Q28 Change management processes
		Q21 Issues related to performance	Q29 Implementation very easy or very difficult
		Q23 Issues related to project management processes	Q30 Time for implementation
		Q25 Standardization of project management processes: not enough or too much	
		Q26 Other issues	
		Q27 Other impacts	

Construct	PMO structure before the transformation	PMO structure after the transformation	Outcomes of change
Items	Q31 Functions	Q32 Functions	Q18 Impacts related to organizational context
	Q33 Supportive and/or Controlling	Q34 Supportive and/or Controlling	Q20 Impacts related to human relations
	Q35 Location within the organization	Q36 Location within the organization	Q22 Impacts related to performance
	Q37a Interdependence between PMOs	Q37b Interdependence between PMOs	Q24 Impacts related to project management processes
	Q38 Merger or division of PMOs		
	Q39 Access to top management	Q40 Access to top management	
	Q41a Number of projects executed simultaneously	Q41b Number of projects executed simultaneously	
	Q42a % of projects	Q42b % of projects	
	Q43a % of project managers	Q43b % of project managers	
	Q44a Employee FTE working in PMO	Q44b Employee FTE working in PMO	
		Q45 PMO hierarchical level, higher or lower	
	Q46 Decision-making authority	Q47 Decision-making authority	
	Q48a Employee reporting to PMO's boss (matrix)	Q48b Employee reporting to PMO's boss (matrix)	
	Q49 Funding	Q50 Funding	
	Q51 Organizational culture	Q52 Organizational culture	
	Q53 Accountability for project performance	Q54 Accountability for project performance	

Appendix E   Sample Demographics

	Total	Percentage		Total	Percentage
Organization type			Position of respondents		
Private	104	57.1	PMO managers	43	20.1
Public	74	40.7	Project managers	38	10.9
Non governmental	4	2.2	Consultant	18	9.8
Total	182	100	Senior executives	14	9.8
			Professional in the PMO	14	9.2
PMO Geographical distribution			Others	49	40.2
Canada	74	41.3	Total	176	100
USA	41	22.9			
Sweden	15	8.2	PM maturity level		
Others	49	27.4	Initial level	38	20.9
Total	179	100	Repeatable level	56	30.8
			Defined level	54	29.7
Economic sector			Managed level	25	13.7
Finance, insurance and est.	35	20.1	Optimizing level	9	4.9
Communications	19	10.9	Total	182	100
Manufacturing	17	9.8			
Public administration	17	9.8	Single or multiple customers		
Business services	16	9.2	Single	42	23.1
Others	70	40.20	Multiple	140	76.9
Total	174	100	Total	182	100
Types of deliverables			Internal or external customers		
IS or IT	84	47.5	Internal	119	65.7
New product/service dev.	34	19.2	External	62	34.3
Engineering or construction	30	16.9	Total	181	100
Business processes	16	9			
Total	177	100	Number of people working on a typical project		
			1 to 25	125	68.7
Employees I organization			26 to 100	48	26.3
1 to 500	43	23.8	More than 101	9	5.0
501 to 1000	13	7.2	Total	182	100
1000 to 10,000 employees	55	30.4			
10,001 to 30,000 employees	30	16.6			
More than 30,000	40	22.1			
Total	181	100			

Appendix F   Factor Correlation Matrix

	1	2	3	4	5	6	7	8	9	10	11
Conditions											
(1) FACT_COND1 External	1										
(2) FACT_COND2 Change in top mgt.	0	1									
Issues											
(3) FACT_ISSUE1 Portfolio mgt. & methods	0.069	0.180*	1								
(4) FACT_ISSUE2 Collaboration & accountability	0.200**	0.122	0	1							
(5) FACT_ISSUE3 PM maturity & performance	0.052	-0.193**	0	0	1						
(6) FACT_ISSUE4 Work climate	**0.393******	0.079	0	0	0	1					
Changes											
(7) FACT_CHANGE1 PM functions & supportiveness	0.207**	-0.128	-0.024	0.076	0.147	0.032	1				
(8) FACT_CHANGE2 Scope of control mandate	0.166*	0.020	0.108	0.264***	-0.003	0.108	0	1			
(9) FACT_CHANGE3 PMO autonomy	0.199**	-0.024	0.285***	0.164	-0.076	0.100	0	0	1		
Impacts											
(10) FACT_IMPAC1 Portfolio mgt. & method	0.002	-0.010	**0.556******	-0.044	0.127	0.161*	**0.344******	0.039	0.236**	1	
(11) FACT_IMPAC2 Collaboration, accountability & skill	**0.373******	0.013	0.111	**0.389******	0.307	0.182**	0.256***	0.297***	0.228**	0	1
(12) FACT_IMPAC3 Work climate PMO cost	0.141	0.173*	-0.129	0.195**	-0.123	**0.371******	0.009	0.052	0.125	0	0

Note. Correlation coefficients above 0.34 are in boldface.

*	Correlation is significant at the $P<0.10$ level (two-tailed)
**	Correlation is significant at the $P<0.05$ level (two-tailed)
***	Correlation is significant at the $P<0.01$ level (two-tailed)
****	Correlation is significant at the $P<0.001$ level (two-tailed)

REFERENCES

Anderson, P., & Tushman, M. L. (1990). Technological discontinuities and dominant designs: A cyclical model of technological change. *Administrative Science Quarterly, 35*(4), 604–633.

Aubry, M. (2007). *La performance organisationnelle des Bureaux de projet: Une analyse intersectorielle.* Université du Québec à Montréal, Montréal.

Aubry, M., & Hobbs, B. (in press). A fresh look at the contribution of project management to the organizational performance. *Project Management Journal.*

Aubry, M., Müller, R., Hobbs, B., & Blomquist, T. (in press). Project management offices in transition. *International Journal of Project Management.*

Benko, C., & McFarlan, F. W. (2003). *Connecting the dots: Aligning projects with objectives in unpredictable times.* Boston: Harvard Business School Press.

Bhaskar, R. (1975). *A realistic theory of science.* Leeds, UK: Leeds Book Ltd.

Blomquist, T., & Müller, R. (2006). *Middle managers in program and project portfolio management: Practices, roles and responsibilities.* Newtown Square, PA: Project Management Institute.

Brady, T., Davies, A., & Gann, D. M. (2005). Creating value by delivering integrated solutions. *International Journal of Project Management, 23*(5), 360-365.

Bredillet, C. N. (2007). From the editor: Exploring research in project management: Nine schools of project management research (part 1). *Project Management Journal, 38*(2), 3–4.

Bredillet, C. N. (2008). From the editor: Exploring research in project management: Nine Schools of project management research (part 5). *Project Management Journal, 39*(2), 2.

Bredillet, C. N., Ruiz, P., & Yatim, F. (2008). *Investigating the Development of Project Management: A Time-Distance Analysis Approach of G8, European G6, and Outreach 5 Countries.* Presented at the 2008 PMI Research Conference, Warsaw.

Bresnen, M., Goussevskaia, A., & Swan, J. (2005). Organisational routines, situated learning and processes of change in project-based organizations. *Project Management Journal, 36*(3), 27.

Bridges, D. N., & Crawford, K. J. (2001). *A project office: Where and what type.* Presented at the Project Management Institute Annual Seminars & Symposium, Nashville.

Brown, S. L., & Eisenhardt, K. M. (1997). The art of continuous change: Linking complexity theory and time-paced evolution in relentlessly shifting organizations. *Administrative Science Quarterly, 42*(1), 1–34.

Burns, T., & Stalker, G. M. (1961). *The management of innovation*. London, UK: Tavistock Publications Limited.

Chandler, A. D., Jr. (1962). *Strategy and structure*. Cambridge: MIT Press.

Chandler, A. D., Jr. (1980). The United States: Seedbed of managerial capitalism. In A. D. Chandler, Jr. & H. Daems (Eds.), *Managerial hierarchies: Comparative perspectives on the rise of the modern industrial enterprise* (pp. 9–40). Cambridge, Massachusetts: Harvard University Press.

Ciborra, C. U. (1996). The platform organization: Recombining strategies, structures, and surprises. *Organization Science, 7*(2), 103–118.

Crawford, K. J. (2002). *The strategic project office: A guide for improving organizational performance*. New York: Marcel Dekker.

Crawford, K. J., & Cabanis-Brewin, J. (2006). *Optimizing human capital with a strategic project office: Select, Train, measure, and reward people for organization success*. Boca Raton, FL: Auerbach.

Crawford, L. (2004, May). *Patterns of support for corporate delivery capability*. Presented at Project Management of South Africa (PMSA), Johannesburg, South Africa.

Crawford, L., Cooke-Davies, T. J., Hobbs, B., Labuschagne, L., Remington, K., & Chen, P. (2008). *Situational sponsorship of projects and programs: An empirical review*. Newtown Square, PA: Project Management Institute.

Crawford, L., Hobbs, B., & Turner, R. J. (2005). *Project categorization systems: Aligning capability with strategy for better results*. Newtown Square, PA: Project Management Institute.

Cronbach, L. J. (1951). Coefficient alpha and the internal structure of tests. *Psychometrika, 16*(3), 297–334.

Dai, C. X. Y., & Wells, W. G. (2004). An exploration of project management office features and their relationship to project performance. *International Journal of Project Management, 22*(7), 523–532.

Denzin, N. K., & Lincoln, Y. S. (2000). *Handbook of qualitative research*. London, UK: SAGE Publications.

DiMaggio, P. J., & Powell, W. W. (1983). The Iron Cage Revisited: Institutional isomorphism and collective rationality in organizational fields. *American Sociology Review, 48*(avril), 147-160.

Dinsmore, P. C. (1999). *Winning in business with enterprise project management*. New York: AMACOM.

Dinsmore, P. C., & Cooke-Davies, T. J. (2006). *Right projects done right!: From business strategy to successful project implementation*. San Francisco: Jossey-Bass.

Donaldson, L. (2001). *The contingency theory of organizations* London: Sage.

Donaldson, L. (1996). The normal science of structural contingency theory. In S. Clegg, C. Hardy & W. R. Nord (Eds.), *Handbook of organization studies* (pp. 57–76). London: Sage.

Donaldson, L. (1987). Strategy and structural adjustment and regain fit to performance: In defence of contingency theory. *Journal of Management Studies, 24*(1), 1–24.

Donaldson, L. (1985). Organization Design and the Life-Cycles of Products. *Journal of Management Studies, 22*(1), 25-37.

Dooley, K. J., & Van de Ven, A. H. (1999). Explaining complex organizational dynamics. *Organization Science, 10*(3), 358.

Duggal, J. S. (2001). *Building a next generation PMO.* Presented at PMI 2001 First to the Future, Nashville.

Eisenhardt, K. M. (1989). Building theories from case study research. *Academy of Management Review, 14*(4), 532-550.

Eisenhardt, K. M., & Schoonhoven, C. B. (1996). Resource-based view of strategic alliance formation: Strategic and social effects in entrepreneurial firms. *Organization Science, 7*(2), 136–150.

Englund, R. L., Graham, R. J., & Dinsmore, P. C. (2003). *Creating the project office: A manager's guide to leading organizational change.* San Francisco: Jossey-Bass.

Engwall, M. (2003). No project is an island: Linking projects to history and context. *Research Policy, 32*(5), 789–808.

Fenton, E., & Pettigrew, A. (2000). Theoretical perspectives on new forms of organizing. In E. Fenton & A. Pettigrew (Eds.), *The innovating organization* (pp. 1–46). London: SAGE.

Galbraith, J. R. (2002). Organizing to deliver solutions. *Organizational Dynamics, 31*(2), 194–207.

Giddens, A. (1984). *The constitution of society: Outline of a theory of structuration.*

Goncalves, M. (2006). *Implementing the virtual project management office: Proven strategies for success.* New York: McGraw-Hill.

Greenwood, R., & Hinings, C. R. (1988). Organizational design types, tracks and the dynamics of strategic change. *Organization Studies, 9*(3), 293–316.

Greenwood, R., & Hinings, C. R. (1996). Understanding radical organizational change: Bringing together the old and the new institutionalism. *Academy of Management Review, 21*(4), 1022–1054.

Hair, J. F., Anderson, R. E., Tatham, R. L., & Black, W. C. (1998). *Multivariate data analysis.* Upper Saddle River, NJ: Pearson Prentice Hall.

Hannan, M. T., & Freeman, J. (1984). Structural inertia and organizational change. *American Sociological Review, 49*(2), 149–164.

Hatfield, M. (2008). *Things your PMO is doing wrong.* Newtown Square, PA: Project Management Institute.

Hedlund, G. (1994). A model of knowledge management and the N-Form Corporation. *Strategic Management Journal, 15.*73-90.

Hobbs, B., & Aubry, M. (2007). A multi-phase research program investigating project management offices (PMOs): The result of phase 1. *Project Management Journal, 38*(1), 74–86.

Hobbs, B., & Aubry, M. (2010). *The Project Management Office or PMO: A Quest for Understanding.* Newtown Square, PA: Project Management Institute.

Hobbs, B., & Aubry, M. (in press). What really affects the performance of PMOs. *Project Management Journal.*

Hobbs, B., Aubry, M., & Thuillier, D. (2008). The project management office as an organisational innovation. *International Journal of Project Management, 26*(5), 547–555.

Hobbs, B., & Ménard, P. M. (1993). Organizational choices for project management. In P. C. Dinsmore (Ed.), *The handbook of project management* (pp. 81–108). New York: AMACOM.

Hobday, M. (2000). The project-based organisation: An ideal form for managing complex products and systems? *Research Policy, 29*(7–8), 871–893.

Huemann, M., & Anbari, F. T. (2007). Project auditing: A tool for compliance, governance, empowerment, and improvement. *Journal of the Academy of Business and Economics, 7*(2), 9–17.

Huemann, M., Keegan, A., & Turner, R. J. (2007). Human resource management in the project-oriented company: A review. *International Journal of Project Management, 25*(3), 315–329.

Hughes, P. T. (1987). The evolution of large technological systems. In W. E. Bijker, T. P. Hughes & T. J. Pinch (Eds.), *The social construction of technological systems: New directions in the sociology and history of technology* (pp. 51–81). Cambridge: MIT Press.

Hurt, M., & Thomas, J. L. (2009). Building value through sustainable project management offices. *Project Management Journal, 40*(1), 55–72.

Interthink Consulting. (2002). State of the PMO 2002, consulted November 2004 from http://www.interthink.ca/research/home.html

Jensen, M. C. (2000). *A theory of the firm: Governance, residual claims, and organizational forms.* Cambridge, MA: Harvard University Press.

Kenny, D. A. (2009) Mediation, http://davidakenny.net/cm/mediate.htm accessed November 15, 2009.

Kendall, G. I., & Rollins, S. C. (2003). *Advanced project portfolio management and the PMO: Multiplying ROI at warp speed.* Fort Lauderdale: FL: J. Ross Publishing.

Larson, E. (2004). Project management structures. In P. W. G. Morris & J. K. Pinto (Eds.), *The Wiley guide to managing projects* (pp. 48–66). Hoboken, NJ: John Wiley & Sons, Inc.

Laughlin, R. C. (1991). Environmental disturbances and organizational transitions and transformations: Some alternative models. *Organization Studies, 12*(2), 209–232.

Lévesque, B., Bourque, G. L., & Forgues, É. (2001). *La nouvelle sociologie économique.* Paris: Desclée de Brouwer.

Lewin, K. (1958). Group decisions and social change. In E. E. Maccoby, T. M. Newcomb & E. L. Hartley (Eds.), *Readings in Social Psychology* (pp. 197–211). New York: Henry Holt and Company.

Light, M. (2000). *The Report Office: Teams, processes, and tools.* Stamford, CT: Gartner Group.

Magenau, J. M., & Pinto, J. K. (2004). Power, influence, and negotiation in project management. In P. W. G. Morris & J. K. Pinto (Eds.), *The Wiley Guide to managing projects* (pp. 1033–1060). Hoboken, NJ: Wiley.

March, J. G. (1981). Footnotes to organizational change. *Administrative Science Quarterly, 26*(4), 563–577.

March, J. G. (1991). Exploration and exploitation in organizational learning. *Organization Science, 2*(1), 71–87.

Marsh, D. (2000). The programme and project support office. In R. J. Turner & S. J. Simister (Eds.), *Handbook of project management* (pp. 131–144). Aldershot, England: Gower.

Massini, S., Lewin, A. Y., Numagami, T., & Pettigrew, A. M. (2002). The evolution of organizational routines among large Western and Japanese firms. *Research Policy, 31*(8-9), 1333–1348.

Merriam-Webster (Ed.) (2007). Merriam-Webster's collegiate dictionary (11th ed.). Springfield, MA: Merriam-Webster.

Midler, C. (1994). *L'auto qui n'existait pas*. Paris: InterÉditions.

Miles, R. E., Snow, C. C., Mathews, J. A., Miles, G., & Coleman, H. J., Jr. (1997). Organizing in the knowledge age: Anticipating the cellular form. *The Academy of Management Executive, 11*(4), 7–21.

Miller, D., & Friesen, P. (1984). *Organizations: A quantum view*. Englewood Cliffs: Prentice-Hall.

Miller, D., & Friesen, P. H. (1982). Structural change and performance: Quantum versus piecemeal-incremental approaches. *Academy of Management Journal, 25*(4), 867–892.

Miner, A. S. (1994). Seeking adaptive advantage: Evolutionary theory and managerial action. In J. A. C. Baum & J. V. Singh (Eds.), *Evolutionary dynamics of organizations* (pp. 76–89). Oxford: Oxford University Press.

Mintzberg, H. (1983). *Power in and around organizations*. Englewood Cliffs, NJ: Prentice-Hall.

Mintzberg, H. (1989). *Mintzberg on management: Inside our strange world of organizations*. New York: The Free Press.

Mintzberg, H. (1979). *The structuring of organizations: A synthesis of the research*. Englewood Cliffs, NJ: Prentice-Hall.

Mintzberg, H., & Westley, F. (1992). Cycles of organizational change. *Strategic Management Journal, 13*, 39–59.

Miranda, E. (2003). *Running the successful hi-tech project office*: Arteck House.

Morabito, J., Sack, I., & Bhate, A. (1999). *Modeling organization: Innovative architectures for the 21st century*. Upper Saddle River, NJ: Prentice Hall.

Morgan, G. (1989). *Images de l'organisation* (S. Chevrier-Vouvé & M. Audet, Trans.). Québec: Presses de l'Université Laval.

Morris, P. W. G., & Jamieson, A. (2004). *Translating corporate strategy into project strategy*. Newtown Square, PA: Project Management Institute.

Müller, R., Martinsuo, M., & Blomquist, T. (2008). project portfolio control and portfolio management performance in different contexts. *Project Management Journal, 39*(3), 28–42.

Nohria, N., & Ghoshal, S. (1997). *The differentiated network: Organizing multinational corporations for value creation*: San Francisco: Jossey-Bass.

Nonaka, I. (1990). Redundant, overlapping organization: A Japanese approach. *California Management Review, 32*(3), 27.

Office of Government Commerce (2008). *Portfolio, programme and project offices [P3O]*. London, UK: The Stationary Office [TSO].

Partington, D. (2000). Building grounded theories of management action. *British Journal of Management, 11*(2), 91–102.

Pellegrinelli, S., & Garagna, L. (2009). Towards a conceptualisation of PMOs as agents and subjects of change and renewal. *International Journal of Project Management, 27,* 649–656.

Pellegrinelli, S., Partington, D., Hemingway, C., Mohdzain, Z., & Shah, M. (2007). The importance of context in programme management: An empirical review of programme practices. *International Journal of Project Management, 25*(1), 41–55.

Perry, M. P. (2009). *Business driven PMO setup.* New York: J. Ross Publishing.

Pettigrew, A. M. (1985). *The awakening giant: Continuity and change in Imperial Chemical Industries.* Oxford: Basil Blackwell.

Pettigrew, A. M. (1990). Longitudinal field research on change: Theory and practice. *Organization Science,* 1 (3) 267–292.

Pettigrew, A. M. (2003). Innovative forms of organizing: Progress, performance and process. In A. M. Pettigrew, R. Whittington, L. Melin, C. Sanchez-Runde, F. A. J. Van den Bosch, W. Ruigrok & T. Numagami (Eds.), *Innovative forms of organizing* (pp. 331–351). London, UK: SAGE Publications.

Pettigrew, A. M., Woodman, R. W., & Cameron, K. S. (2001). Studying organizational change and development: Challenges for future research. *Academy of Management Journal, 44*(4), 697.

Powell, W. (1990). Neither market nor hierarchy: Network forms of organization. In B. M. Staw & L. L. Cummings (Eds.), *Research in organizational behavior* (Vol. 12, pp. 295–336).

Project Management Institute. (2008a). *A guide to the project management body of knowledge (PMBOK® guide)* — fourth edition. Newtown Square, PA: Project Management Institute.

Project Management Institute. (2008b). *Organizational project management maturity model (OPM3®) knowledge foundation* (2nd ed.). Newtown Square, PA: Project Management Institute.

Program Management Office Specific Interest Group [PMOSIG]. (2008). *PMO SIG Accord. Project Management Office Specific Interest group.*

Project Management Office Special Interest Group [PMOSIG]. (2010). *PMOSIG Program Management Office Handbook.* Newtown Square, PA: Project Management Institute.

Rajagopalan, N., & Spreitzer, G. M. (1997). Toward a theory of strategic change: A multi-lens perspective and integrative framework. *Academy of Management Review, 22*(1), 48–79.

Roberts, P. W., & Amit, R. (2003). The dynamics of innovative activity and competitive advantage: The case of Australian retail banking, 1981 to 1995. *Organization Science, 14*(2), 107.

Romanelli, E., & Tushman, M. L. (1994). Organizational transformation as punctuated equilibrium: An empirical test. *Academy of Management Journal, 37*(5), 1141–1666.

Ruigrok, W., Pettigrew, A. M., Peck, S., & Whittington, R. (1999). Corporate restructuring and new forms of organizing: Evidence from Europe. *Management International Review, 39,* 41.

Schumpeter, J. (1950). *Capitalism, Socialism, and Democracy* (3rd ed.). New York:

Harper & Row Publishers.

Schwarz, G., & Brock, D. (1998). Waving hello or waving good-bye? Organizational change in the information age. *International Journal of Organizational Analysis, 6*(1), 65–90.

Shenhar, A. J., & Dvir, D. (2004). How projects differ, an what to do about it. In P. W. G. Morris & J. K. Pinto (Eds.), *The Wiley Guide to Managing Projects* (pp. 1265–1286). Hoboken, NJ: John Wiley & Sons, Inc.

Slevin, D. P., & Pinto, J. K. (2004). An overview of behavioral issues in project management. In P. W. G. Morris & J. K. Pinto (Eds.), *The Wiley Guide to managing projects* (pp. 67–85). Hoboken, NJ: Wiley.

Sminia, H. (2009). Process research in strategy formation: Theory, methodology and relevance. *International Journal of Management Reviews, 11*(1), 97–125.

Stanleigh, M. (2005). *The impact of implementing a project management office: Report on the results of the on-line survey*: Business Improvement Architects.

Strauss, A. L., & Corbin, J. (1990). *Basics of qualitative research grounded theory procedures and techniques*. Newbury Park, CA: Sage.

Strauss, A. L., & Corbin, J. (1998). *Basics of qualitative research: Techniques and procedures for developing grounded theory* (2nd ed.). Thousand Oaks, CA: Sage.

Thomas, J. L., & Mullaly, M. E. (2008). *Researching the value of project management*. Newtown Square, PA: Project Management Institute.

Thompson, J. D. (1967). *Organizations in action*. New York: McGraw-Hill.

Turner, J. R., & Müller, R. (2006). *Choosing appropriate project managers: Matching their leadership style to the type of project*. Newtown Square, PA: Project Management Institute.

Tushman, M. L., & Romanelli, E. (1985). Organizational evolution: A metamorphosis model of convergence and reorientation. In L. L. Cummings & B. M. Staw (Eds.), *Research in organizational behavior* (Vol. 7, pp. 171–222). Greenwich, CT: JAI Press.

Van de Ven, A. H. (2007). *Engaged Scholarship: Creating knowledge for science and practice*. Oxford: Oxford University Press.

Van de Ven, A. H. (1999). *The innovation journey*. New York: Oxford University Press.

Van de Ven, A. H., & Garud, R. (1994). The co-evolution of technical and institutional events in the development of an innovation. In J. A. C. Baum & J. V. Singh (Eds.), *Evolutionary dynamics of organizations* (pp. 425–443). New York: Oxford University Press.

Van de Ven, A. H., & Poole, M. S. (1995). Explaining development and change in organizations. *Academy of Management Review, 20*, 510–540.

Van de Ven, A. H., & Poole, M. S. (2005). Alternative approaches for studying organizational change. *Organization Studies, 26*(9), 1377–1404.

Vargo, S. L., & Lusch, R. F. (2004). Evolving to a new dominant logic for marketing. *Journal of Marketing, 68*(1), 1–17.

Weick, K. E., & Quinn, R. E. (1999). Organizational change and development. *Annual Review of Psychology, 50*(1), 361–386.

Williams, T. (2005). Assessing and moving on from the dominant project management discourse in the light of project overruns. *IEEE Transactions on*

Engineering Management, 52(4), 497–508.

Winter, M. & Szczepanek, T. (2009). *Images of projects.* Gower Publishing, Cornwall, UK.

Yin, R. K. (2003). *Case study research: Design and methods* (3rd ed.). London, UK: SAGE Publications.

Zeitlin, J. (2008). The historical alternatives approach. In G. Jones & J. Zeitlin (Eds.), *The Oxford handbook of business history* (pp. 120–140). Oxford: Oxford University Press.